Media, Conflict and Peace in Northeast India

Media, Conflict and Peace in Northeast India

Edited by

Dr. Kh. Kabi
Dr. S N. Pattnaik

Foreword by

Paranjoy Guha Thakurta

Y

Vij Books India Pvt Ltd
New Delhi (India)

Published by

Vij Books India Pvt Ltd
(Publishers, Distributors & Importers)
2/19, Ansari Road
Delhi – 110 002
Phones: 91-11-43596460, 91-11-47340674
Fax: 91-11-47340674
e-mail: vijbooks@rediffmail.com

Copyright © 2015,

ISBN: 978-93-84464-75-2

Content

Foreword

The northeastern part of India comprising the 'seven sisters' or states of Assam, Arunachal Pradesh, Nagaland, Manipur, Meghalaya, Mizoram and Tripura, together with the eighth state of Sikkim, is separated from the rest of the country by a narrow 'chicken's neck' near Siliguri, in the northern part of West Bengal—a land corridor that is physically just 29 km wide. More than geographical separation, sections of people in the northeast have for long felt 'alienated' from India's political, social and economic mainstream.

The northeast has around four per cent of India's population living in eight per cent of the country's geographical area. This region is surrounded by four countries: Bangladesh, Bhutan, China and Myanmar. Ninety-six per cent of the borders of the northeastern region of India are international boundaries. A slew of questions relating to sub-nationalism, regional and ethnic identities, illegal immigration and violent separatist movements have dominated much of the discourse on the north-east, which is arguably one of the most heterogeneous parts of the world.

The longest lasting insurgency has been that of the Nagas who declared 'independence' a day before India did, that is, on August 14, 1947. In 1963, Nagaland was the first of four states to be carved out of undivided Assam, but the demands for independence, autonomy, cease-fire and territorial expansion have continued in different forms. Negotiations have taken place between and among various central and state agencies of the Indian government and groups like the National Socialist Council of Nagaland (Isak-Muivah) or NSCN(I-M) and the NSCN (Khaplang). The main demand of the NSCN(I-M) is for a 'greater' Nagaland, including the contiguous Naga majority districts in the neighbouring state of Manipur.

With the possible exception of the United Liberation Front of Asom (ULFA), which demands independence for Assam, the remaining groups demanding independence in Tripura and Manipur have done so intermittently in recent years. One of the major grievances of these groups relates to the failure of the Union government to protect the demographic and cultural 'integrity' of ethnic groups from those considered legal as well as illegal migrants. A number of smaller groups represent particular minorities and demand greater separate statehood or greater autonomy through protection under the Sixth Schedule of the Constitution of India, of the kind granted to the Bodos in Assam. Among the 'seven sisters', Arunachal Pradesh and—to a lesser extent—Meghalaya have not had major long-standing insurgent movements seeking independence or greater autonomy, while Mizoram is the only state in the region which has been governed in a relatively stable manner by former insurgents and violence has almost completely abated in recent years.

At the time of Independence, the northeast was one of the most prosperous regions in the whole of India. Six and half decades later, this area has become one of the most troubled and backward regions in the country. In 1947, undivided Assam had the second highest per capita income among all states in India. After the 1965 India-Pakistan war, transit facilities between the north-east and West Bengal through Bangladesh (then East Pakistan) were denied. Subsequently, the northeastern part of India started witnessing problems associated with land-locked regions. Before 1947, the distance between Guwahati and Kolkata would be less than 600 km against 1,300 km at present; the distance between Agartala and Kolkata would be 350 km against 2,000 km now.

In many parts of the north-east, over-dependence on funds from the Union government has incubated powerful and corrupt elites. Until local groups with the help of the media address the issue of corruption by exerting pressure from below to ensure greater transparency on the part of politicians and officials, the future development of the region will be severely constrained. However, it is also true that economic considerations do not fully explain the myriad problems of the peoples of this part of the planet. Despite huge financial programmes that have been formulated and expended—there is a separate ministry in the government of India called the Ministry for Development of the North-Eastern Region (or DONER)—identity issues stemming from ethnic, linguistic, religious and cultural differences have sometimes proved more difficult to resolve and become intractable.

The northeast is certainly not all about violence and insurgency. The area has traditions of community-based economic and social organizations and an amazingly rich cultural repertoire. Nagaland's experience of 'communitization' is acknowledged as an exemplar for the country. The northeast depends heavily on agriculture. There is considerable potential for horticulture, floriculture and cultivation of medicinal plants. Besides traditional crops like tea, there is scope for developing plantations for bamboo, rubber, spices and fruits. The northeast has amazing forest wealth, bio-diversity and genetic resources. Arunachal Pradesh is considered to be one of the world's most important ecological hotspots.

Yet, Mother Nature also causes many problems. Controlling the impact that floods cause is a major task, especially in Assam. Large dams have become increasingly unfeasible for social, environmental and technical reasons and there is need to focus on small and medium irrigation projects. Yet, under pressure from powerful lobbies of contractors with support from their political mentors, a number of major hydro-electric projects have been envisaged that have the potential of disrupting the fragile ecology of the region. Information technology and education have huge possibilities for generating productive employment in the region. But, implementation of plans and projects remains painfully slow.

This volume of essays seeks to highlight different facets of the role of the mass media in not merely reporting on conflict situations but also in facilitating and enabling peaceful conditions in this region. The articles and papers have been compiled by some of the finest reporters and analysts of the complex realities of north-eastern India. The writers look at issues in a nuanced manner. Journalists are on occasions caught in the crossfire between security forces and insurgent groups. On other occasions, they become, willy-nilly, participants and players in larger political and social processes. This book looks at various aspects of reporting what is happening in this part of the world and explaining situations that are prevailing to wider audiences in India and across the world. These are often extremely difficult tasks and living up to the challenges posed, is easier said than done.

Media persons working in the northeast have often had to face direct and indirect threats of violence from non-state as well as state actors. Freedom of expression acquires very different connotations to those who seek to communicate to large numbers of people in this region. To report and document ethnic cleansing, killing and torture of dissidents and government agents, kidnapping, abduction, extortion, sabotage and violence against innocent women and children (including rape and molestation) is not a simple task in the best of times. What makes the work for journalists here even more challenging is to situate such sporadic events in their wider contexts of economic deprivation and environmental degradation.

The book compiles essays that deal with the problems of the peoples of the north-east in a holistic manner. Bert Lintner is a Chiang Mai (Thailand)-based journalist, who is married to a Shan from Myanmar. His article on the media and ethnic conflicts is based on his experiences as a journalist who has covered insurgencies not only in the northeast but also in Myanmar for more than three decades. Haroon Habib, a one-time guerrilla fighter, brings the Bangladesh perspective into his essay, while Darshana Liyanage makes a comparative study of advertising and ethnicities in Sri Lanka and northeast India. Monalisa Changkija, editor and publisher of an English daily published from Nagaland, *The Nagaland Page*, writes on the media as facilitators of peace.

Award-winning journalist Teresa Rehman, who is founding editor of the website, *www.thethumbprintmag.com*, draws on her professional experience in reporting on the impact of militancy on the most vulnerable sections of society—the disabled, women, children and the elderly—and on welfare programmes related to health-care, education and employment. Senior journalists and authors Samudra Gupta Kashyap of the *Indian Express*, Nirendra Dev of *The Statesman* and Rajeev Bhattacharya make valuable contributions on the media coverage of peace and conflict situations that go beyond their personal perspectives. Samir K. Purkayastha, who is a journalist as well as a scholarly writer, focuses on the role of the media in enforcing change in his essay. Last, but certainly not the least, Pradip Phanjoubam, founder editor of the English daily, *Imphal Free Press,* who has been a fellow at the Indian Institute of Advanced Study, Shimla, and has written and commented extensively on the northeast, has placed before readers a particularly perceptive and reflective account on trauma reporting and conflict resolution.

- Paranjoy Guha Thakurta

...

Contributors

Foreword by : Paranjoy Guha Thakurta

Paranjoy Guha Thakurta is an independent journalist, political commentator, author and a documentary film maker. He is also a regular guest lecturer at some of the top institutes like the Indian Institutes of Management, Jawaharlal Nehru University and Jamia Millia Islamia. Through his career spanning over 38 years, he has been associated with major media houses like Business India, Businessworld, The Telegraph, India Today and The Pioneer. He also hosted the chat show India Talks on CNBC-India which ran over 1400 episodes. His latest book is titled *Gas Wars: Crony Capitalism and Ambanis.*

About the Authors

Bertil Lintner is the former correspondent with *Far Eastern Economic Review* and currently Asia Correspondent for the Swedish daily, *Sevenksa Dagbladet* as well as contributor to *Asia Times* online, Hong Kong and *Jane's Information Group* in the UK. He has written thirteen books on Asian politics and history, among them are *Outrage: Burma Struggle for Democracy*; *Land of Jade: A journey from India through Northern Burma and China*; and *Great Games East: India, China and the Struggle for Asia's Most Volatile Frontier.* He lives in Chiang Mai, Thailand.

Haroon Habib is a senior journalist, writer and columnist, remains a powerful voice in journalism, creative writings and social activism in Bangladesh. A guerrilla fighter in the Bangladesh's Liberation War, Haroon Habib simultaneously worked from the warfront for the *Joy Bangla* weekly and *Swadhin Bangla Beter Kendra* radio, two powerful mouthpieces of the war-time Bangladesh government that had led the country's Liberation War in 1971. Haroon Habib led the country's national news agency *Bangladesh*

Sangbad Sangsthas as its Chief Editor and Managing Director and served for over two decades as Dhaka Correspondent of India's prestigious English daily *The Hindu* and *Frontline* magazine. He also worked as Stringer of *Time* magazine, and worked for several years as Bangladesh Correspondent of the Bengali Service of the German Radio *Deutsche Welle*. He is currently the Acting Secretary General of the *Sector Commanders' Forum*, the pioneering national organization of the 1971 war veterans that has been campaigning for war crimes trial. Mr. Habib also leads *Journalism and Peace Foundation,* an organization he founded for promoting peace and social harmony. Mr. Habib is the recipient of prestigious *Bangla Academy Award* for 2013 for his contribution in the Bangla literature.

Monalisa Changkija is the editor and publisher of *The Nagaland Page,* an English daily published from the State of Nagaland in Northeast India.

Pradip Phanjoubam is the founder editor of *Imphal Free Press,* an English daily published from Imphal. He was also a Fellow at the Indian Institute of Advanced Study, Shimla, from May 2011 to May 2014, to research on the geopolitics which shaped the northeast India during the 19th and the 20th centuries. He has written extensively on northeast issues in numerous national publications, including the *Economic and Political Weekly, The Times of India, The Economics Times, The Hindu* and *The Telegraph,* among others.

Samir K Purkayastha is an independent writer and journalist based in Kolkata. He has worked in various capacities in *The Telegraph, The Asian Age, The Sentinel, The Seven Sisters Post, The Nagaland Page,* and *The Nagaland Observers.* He has written several research papers in scholarly journals and books. Some of his recent publications include *UID's Augean Task?; Assam and Illegal Migrants;* and *Consequences of Long-term Conflicts in Northeast India: Impact on Assam, Mizoram, Meghalaya,* and *Tripura.*

Teresa Rehman is an award-winning journalist based in northeast India. She started her career with *India Today* magazine in New Delhi. After a brief sojourn in Delhi, she returned to her roots and has been consistently trying to highlight the myriad hues of this hitherto unexplored and conflict-torn region of the country. She has worked on pertinent issues like impact of militancy on women and children, health, education, rural employment and the disabled. She has won accolades for her work. She has been awarded with the *WASH Media Awards* 2009-2010 in the English category for her work on water supply, sanitation and hygiene journalism by the Water Supply and Sanitation Collaborative Council and the Stockholm International Water Institute. She was honoured with the *Ramnath Goenka Excellence in Journalism Award* for two consecutive years (2008-09 and 2009-10) for the category 'Reporting on Jammu and Kashmir and the Northeast. She was earlier awarded the *Sanskriti Award* 2009 for Excellence in Journalism and the *Seventh Sarojini Naidu Prize* 2007 for Best Reporting on Panchayati Raj by The Hunger Project (*www. thp.org*). She was also honoured with the *Kunjabala Devi Memorial Award* for investigative journalism on women's issues by *The Assam Tribune* group in 2003. Currently Teresa Rehman is the founding editor of the webzine www.thethumbprintmag.com (*The Thumb Print*).

Samudra Gupta Kashyap is a veteran journalist and assistant editor of *The Indian Express* based in Guwahati. He has been reporting the Northeast for more than three decades now.

Rajeev Bhattacharyya is a senior journalist based in Guwahati. He was the founding executive editor of Seven Sisters Post and had earlier worked for *The Times of India, The Telegraph, The Indian Express* and *Times Now.* His published books are *Lens and the Guerrilla: Insurgency in India's Northeast* and *Rendezvous with Rebels: Journey to Meet India's Most Wanted Men.*

Nirendra Dev is the special representative with *The Statesman* in New Delhi and author of the book *The Talking Guns: Northeast India* and *Modi to Moditva: An Uncensored Truth* among others. He blogs at: www. bestofindiarestofindia.blogspot.com

Darshana Liyanage is a senior faculty in the Department of Sinhala at the University of Ruhuna, Sri Lanka

The Media and Ethnic Conflicts

BERTIL LINTNER

For those of you who are not familiar with my work, it helps to know that I have covered ethnic conflicts in Myanmar for more than three decades and I have also written quite extensively on insurgencies in India's northeast. Some of you may be familiar with my book *Great Game East: India, China and the Struggle for Asia's Most Volatile Frontier*, in which I look at the ethnic insurgencies in the Northeast in a geopolitical context. In 1985 I and my wife, who is a Shan from Myanmar, entered the state of Nagaland without any official permission, stayed there for nearly four months—also without any permit to do so—and then crossed the border into Myanmar.

We spent two and a half months in an area controlled by the then undivided National Socialist Council of Nagaland (NSCN) before the camp where we stayed was attacked by Myanmar government forces. I did survive, as you can see, and we were able to continue our trek east, to Myanmar's Kachin State, where we spent almost a year in areas controlled by the Kachin Independence Army. While we were there, we had the opportunity to meet with, and interview, rebels from Manipur. We had already met some of them, and the leadership of the United Liberation Front of Assam (ULFA) while we were in the Naga Hills.

From Kachin State in the north we trekked south into Shan State, were we spent six months in an area controlled by the now defunct Communist Party of Burma (CPB). After more than a year and a half inside insurgent held areas in Myanmar, we entered China illegally. We were detained there for a week or so, and then deported to Hong Kong. From there we flew home to Thailand, where we live.

But even long before this long trek, more than 2,200 kilometres, through northern and northeastern Myanmar, I had trekked across the border into Myanmar from the Thai side and spent some time with Shan, Karen, Karenni, Mon and Pa-O rebel armies. I have also visited rebel camps and villages in southeastern Bangladesh near that countries border with Myanmar, and, in the early 1990s, I travelled into the Chittagong Hill Tracts, where native Chakmas were resisting Bengali dominance.

It is not an easy task for a journalist to write about any war. It is obviously not possible to go back and forth between two warring parties, so one has to stay on one side of the conflict. But, as I wrote in *Land of Jade*, my book about our long trek through northern Myanmar in 1985-1987, "My desire has always been to be as objective and factual as possible—and to describe the war from the point of view of all the innocent people who are affected by it rather than glorifying the various armies involved." And that, to me, remains the best way to promote a better understanding of ethnic, social and political conflicts.

Some people talk about "peace journalism", but to me, that is a dangerous approach to the kind of conflicts I have covered and am still covering. If you set that as an objective, to "promote peace", it is very easy to become biased, to filter information and write only about what you think may serve the purpose of establishing peace in a conflict area. In other words, to suppress unpleasant news and highlight only what appears to be positive developments. That, I'm afraid, leads to distorted views of reality, because the truth is not always pleasant and what we would like to hear or read. It would also be counterproductive to the efforts of those interested in solving ethnic and social conflicts. And then, how do we define peace? It may mean different things to different people. What an authoritarian regime calls peace may be perceived as repression by its subjects.

As I see it, the duty of us journalists is to be as objective as possible, and, in the words of Adolph Ochs, once the owner of the *New York Times*, "to give the news impartially, without fear or favour, regardless of party, sect, or interests involved". Then, and only then, can we journalist be seen as doing our job as real professionals. And only when the truth has been exposed and explained impartially can different parties in an ethnic or social conflict sit down and solve their differences.

I have stated that it is not possible to go back and forth between two warring parties and that one has to stay on one side of an armed conflict. That leaves us journalists with two challenges: first, how do we get the other side of the story? And then, what do we do if we find that the warring party we are with commits atrocities and behaves in a way that a sound human being would find outrageous?

Well, we can always get the other side of the story later, when we are back at our respective bases. But some may not talk to us because we have been with their "enemy" and, therefore, believe that we are also enemies. That, however, can usually be overcome. It becomes more difficult when a rebel army, which has put up with our presence for weeks or even months, expect us to write only their side of the story. If we don't, we can easily be accused of "abusing their hospitality." That has happened to me several times. When I was in the eastern Naga Hills, across the border in Myanmar, it didn't take long before I was appalled by the way in which the Indian Nagas treated the Myanmar Nagas. I witnessed people being beaten and forced to become porters for the NSCN's rebel army. I heard of executions of villagers who had resisted the NSCN's attempts to take over their homeland. I was also told of bloody purges within the organisation.

I had to write about that as well as the religious fanaticism I came across. The outcome of that was that the NSCN "banned" my book *Land of Jade*. Of course, they had to authority to do so, but it meant that its followers were not allowed to read it. Why? The truth was probably too unpleasant even for the NSCN's leadership. But in 1988, three years after we had left the NSCN's base area across the border, the Myanmar Nagas rose up against the organisations leaders and drove them out of Myanmar. This came as no surprise to me, and anyone who has read *Land of Jade* would understand why that uprising took place. It is our duty as journalists and writers to provide that kind of information, even it if is unpleasant things we write about and even if we become unpopular with our former hosts. As I see it, is the duty of us journalists who venture into areas where there is ethnic and civil strife to tell the truth.

The situation was very similar in the area then controlled by the Communist Party of Burma. They wanted me to become "the Edgar Snow" of Myanmar and, presumably, write a book along the lines of "Red Star over Myanmar." I didn't. Instead, I wrote about how the ethnic Bamar leaders of the CPB used the hill tribe population under their control as cannon fodder in their fight against the Myanmar government's army. I wrote about how outdated the CPB's policies were. They were stuck in the days of China's Cultural Revolution. Not surprisingly, the CPB leaders were furious when I write about all this in two cover stories for the magazine I wrote for in those days, the *Far Eastern Economic Review,* in May and June 1987. But then, in March and April 1989, a mutiny broke out in the CPB's army. The hilltribe rank and file drove the old leaders into exile in China. Even the Chinese were becoming sick and tired of the CPB and its inability to adjust to changing times. When I met some of those former CPB leaders in exile in Yunnan in China, they actually admitted that I had been right and that they should have taken what I wrote more seriously.

When I have been, physically that is, on the side of a conflict, I have had similar problems. In March 1990, I was actually invited by the Bangladesh government to visit the Chittagong Hill Tracts to see the progress that was being made in implementing a new autonomy scheme for that area. I told my editors in at *Far Eastern Economic Review* in Hong Kong that I would only accept that invitation if I also could visit the Chakma refugee camps in Tripura. I did go to the Chittagong Hill Tracts, flew around with a Bangladesh army commander and met local people in the presence of him and others from the Bangladeshi military. I did not tell him or my Bangladeshi hosts that I was also going to the refugee camps — but that was what I did when I had left Bangladesh and travelled to India, first to Kolkata then to Agartala. The outcome was what I consider an objective account of the conflict in the Chittagong Hill Tracts. But the Bangladeshi authorities were not pleased, I had betrayed their hospitality and, the next time I applied for a visa for Bangladesh, it was refused. It was only after the Swedish embassy in Dhaka had asked for an explanation from the Bangladeshi authorities that they, reluctantly, agreed to issue me with a visa. It was 1991 and I was then going to cover the influx of Rohingya refugees to Bangladesh, which I also did.

So, to sum it up, we journalists are not especially popular in certain quarters. But I am old-fashioned enough to believe that we have an important role to fill in conflict areas. And that role is to report objectively, factually, and without bias—other than deep consideration for all the innocent people who are affected by the conflicts we cover. We are often accused of fanning conflicts by reporting what could be detrimental to peace. But don't shoot the messenger. In the long run, the truth is always the strongest weapon for solving conflicts. And it is my duty as a journalist, and now also as an author, to present you, to the best of my ability, with that truth. It is my hope that my reports and analyses will help people in conflict areas see their problems more clearly, and find ways to solve them. But how that should be done is up to them, not to me. I am, after all, a reporter and, hopefully, also an educator, not a peace activist.

Media, Peace and Conflict: Northeast India and Bangladesh

HAROON HABIB

The subject of media, peace and conflict is important for all of us in the region due to the turmoil and conflicts we have been experiencing, and for all who want the media to play a constructive role in covering conflicts, and also not inciting but reducing tension as possible as they can. As a media practitioner from a next door neighbour, Bangladesh, I had the privilege of witnessing, somewhat closely, the developments of this region for long four decades, I have readily accepted the invitation to be here amongst you. This will enrich my understanding of the issue, and, of course, allow me to make a few points.

The conflicts in Africa, Afghanistan, Iraq and Syria, and very recently the alarm spread world over with the emergence of ISIS or the 'Islamic State' comprising parts of Syria and Iraq, have no comparison with this region, the India's northeast, in terms of characters and magnitude. However, India's northeast, which share borders with a number of countries, has its own characteristics due to its diversity of races, religions and languages.

The northeast has a large number of ethnic communities, tribal and non-tribal groups, and their living had many a times marred by mutual rivalries. In the past decades, we have seen that besides inter-ethnic clashes, the conflicts in northeast even ranged from struggle for 'autonomy' or 'independence'. Some of these groups have already given up arms to emerge as legitimate political parties. Some still are demanding their 'own homeland' or rights. Therefore, the problems in the northeast are quite different than those of others.

Since northeast has borders with Bangladesh, Myanmar, Bhutan, and China, the region has certain amount of extra problems. This linkage, however, has widened its scopes to explore potentials and derive benefits for all who live in and outside the international borders.

Media in Conflict Situation

Media play an increasingly important role in today's world; they shape and re-shape the peoples mind. I am an ardent advocate of the freedom of the media, and believe unhindered freedom of media has no alternative in a democracy. Nevertheless, no freedom is absolute; therefore, media must protect the people's right to know the right. In saying so, I would equally say that journalists working in all news media: print, television or in other electronic outlets must maintain their ethical standard. Examples are many that a section of the media function irresponsibly, incited in inflammatory manner and even contributed to fuel conflict. Journalists have powerful weapons. Their weapon must be used judiciously.

The violent conflicts all over the world have changed their characters. It is not always the war between states now, but increasingly among the people, between communities and other interests within the common borders. In many places, they are also a terrifying exploitation of civilians and by soldiers or paramilitary forces or private armies. With new technologies expanding, the media is also increasingly the target for misinformation, manipulation or even suppression by various interest groups who would like to profit from such violence.

Innumerable journalists around the world have been killed, injured or imprisoned while covering armed conflicts. They are increasingly becoming targets of war-mongers because media has the potential to influence the course of conflict resolution.

Despite such risks, journalists cannot avoid covering conflicts. Media operations in the non-conflict zones are altogether different from the media function in a troubled periphery. What needs to be done is to understand the dynamics of conflict, and its instigation, development and resolution. Because in many places around the globe, many journalists are accused of finding themselves ill-equipped to address the issue which demands so much of their careful attention.

The fundamental role of the news media is to serve the public interest by being a reliable information provider. However, since journalism has social responsibility, many practitioners believe their work can help make the world a better place.

Technological advances gave the electronic media an astonishing global capability to reach most remote places. It is, therefore, essential for raising professional standard and capacity-building in journalism utilizing ethical standard.

There are some basis elements in reporting conflict which are widely accepted.

1. Increased appreciation of essential professional standards;

2. Strengthening the capacity to analyze conflict;

3. Strengthening the capacity to make conflict sources, processes and possible solution more transparent to society;

4. Increasing awareness of the influence of reporting techniques upon resolving conflict;

5. Strengthening reporting skills in use of speeches and language;

6. Avoidance of hate speech; and

7. Strengthening awareness of gender issues and establishing gender balance in reporting.

Reducing the Conflict

In the recent years, the world has witnessed an increasing role of the news media in reporting conflicts, caused by political turmoil, ethnic or religious conflict or by armed aggression. Therefore, media's role has received a good deal of public attention. Policy makers, social scientists and journalists all point to that important role as the antagonists seek to promote their own interests by influencing the media.

Under the situation, journalists, academics and peace researchers discussed a new practice of reporting that works for peace and engages reporters in the roles of advocacy. But that initiative puts at risk by those who prefer traditional role of journalism.

In fact, a new trend has emerged in the 1980s to use journalism in conflict-reduction. The thinking has found more ground after the fall of the Berlin Wall and when a section of the media were blamed for sparking genocide in Rwanda. Many people then badly felt the need to develop free but responsible media. It is therefore, essential to strictly adhere to the core values or standard of journalism: accuracy, objectivity, ethical conduct, and free from outside influences. If this standard is followed, I have all the faith that media can play a significant role in the reduction of conflict.

Peace Building

Media does not independently direct the course a conflict. But news media can play a meaningful role in creating conducive conditions for conflict resolution. In the early media initiatives, the words 'peace building' rarely came up. Gradually such peace building effort has started getting stronger with the exploration of the media's newer potentials. However, the question is: can media build peace or influence public towards non-violent conflict resolution?

No denying the fact that media can be an 'instrument' of conflict resolution when the information it presents is reliable, respects human rights, and represents diverse views. True journalism supports the people to rebuild peaceful society and to reduce conflict, and not accelerate conflict and violence. Therefore, true journalism can help society live peacefully, and move toward democratic values. Nevertheless, by itself, the media cannot end conflict.

However, there is a major ethical issue raised: will peace journalism or conflict-reduction journalists remain impartial? Critics claim that journalists with a pre-conceived mission cannot be impartial if their primary aim is to build social stability or promote peace. They say, objectivity in journalism will be compromised to obtain desired a social outcome. Keeping peace building or conflict-resolution in mind, they claim, journalists will have to compromise controversial facts and overlook tough issues.

However, proponents of the idea defend that conflict reduction is not served by censoring voices, slanting the evidence and hiding uncomfortable facts, but to see whether ultimate good of the society is maintained. This section also does not consider news as mere commodity for sale, or journalism a mere trade. So debate goes on.

I am a strong proponent of journalism for a mission to serve the society. However, I equally believe that being attached to peace building is not enough. How one carries out such work is also important. While covering conflict, media practitioners should look to the common good, question inaccurate statements and avoid provocative or malicious language. This helps defuse escalation of conflict. Here, I would stress on advancement of ethical standards of journalism, and believe this can be done best through discussion, research and teaching.

In fact, peace journalism, as I see it, is a responsible way of journalism aimed at serving the society. The International Principles of Ethics in Journalism adopted in the 1983 UNESCO consultative meeting of journalism organizations stated that a "true journalist stands for ... peace, democracy, human rights... and participates actively and contributes through dialogue to a climate ... conducive of peace and justice everywhere."

I am also aware about criticism as many people would describe peace journalism as simple abandonment of the integrity of journalism. They argue that peace journalism "is simply not the role of a journalist and is based on the flawed notion." But journalism not only informs, but also educate. Therefore, its peace-building role cannot be overlooked.

Peace journalism combines journalism with an added aim. It is more responsible media coverage of conflict aims at contributing to serving peace, and not making benefit out of aggravated crisis.

Bangladesh and India's Northeast

The relation of Bangladesh with India's northeast was not congenial when Pakistan's eastern part was existed. When the former East Pakistan emerged as an independent entity through a devastating war in 1971, the state of relations with India had radically changed. But the desired warmth got setback when the Bangladesh's Founding Father, Sheikh Mujibur Rahman, was assassinated in 1975 and the country took a reverse turn from its Pro-1971 stand, the national mood that had inspired the nation to fight the genocidal Pakistan army and their local Islamist cohorts. Unfortunately, the post-1975 trend continued for nearly two decades, till 1996. Therefore, there was no substantive move to explore the potentials.

Now the situation has greatly changed. Political will in both the country has emerged to look for cooperation. Major independent media outlets in Bangladesh are in support of building closer relations with India, specially with the northeast, for shared benefit.

In the changed atmosphere, the northeast states of India and Bangladesh are looking for more cooperation in trade, commerce and investment. During the previous Congress-led government some major steps were taken. Those were possible because the Awami League-led secular and pro-liberation politics is in the helm of affairs for quite some time.

It was debated in Bangladesh that the BJP government led by Prime Minister Narendra Modi might change their policies since it was initiated by the Congress. But it did not happen. During Sushma Swaraj's first stand-alone visit to Dhaka as India's new External Affairs Minister in June 2014, she sought to remove the trust deficit.

This followed the visit of Gen. V K Singh who is also the Union Minister for Development of Northeastern Region. Singh's delegation included top political and business people and the government leaders from the northeast. Trade and commerce, besides the long-felt connectivity, were the main topics of discussion during Gen Singh's visit.

There is plenty of scope to expand Bangladesh's trade with the India's northeast. It is widely accepted that the economies of both India and Bangladesh can benefit immensely with enhanced bilateral trade and investments. India-Bangladesh trade is increasing over the years, but the balance of trade is heavily tilted towards India. This needs to be looked into.

Journalists do not only report violence, sensation or conflict but educate people towards peaceful, collective and congenial living. They shape and re-shape public mind to remove legacies of mistrust and age-old mental barriers. Therefore, it is important for journalists on both sides of the border to concentrate on their ethical standards and go for balanced media coverage.

For the northeastern states, Bangladesh is the next-door neighbor. They need Bangladesh for connecting with the rest of India quickly and easily. Bangladesh, too, needs the northeast for expanding trade and commerce.

Bangladesh, during past few years, has met some vital security concerns of the India's northeast. Transshipment through Bangladesh to northeast is already in progress. Transit through Bangladesh is gradually becoming a reality. However, Bangladesh is still looking for India to honour its two major commitments: The Teesta Water-Sharing Treaty and Ratification of the Land Boundary Agreement, singed in 1974, to allow the two countries to exchange land enclaves. The two should not remain pending for indefinite period.

I would admit it is not always simple to resolve all the issues over night. Assam has a problem with 'illegal Bangladeshi migrants'. The local public mood is stated to be against transfer of enclaves, and also against ratification of the Land Boundary Agreement. Therefore, a consensus is needed to be achieved. Media on both sides of the border should look into these issues in greater regional perspectives; not entirely on patriotic basis, but on historic and ground realities. The humanitarian aspect of these issues must not get less attention.

In Bangladesh, a growing mood was noticed in the recent years that the two next-door neighbours should take advantage of their geographical proximity. Bangladesh is becoming an attractive investment destination for Indian entrepreneurs who have already invested 2.5 billion dollar there. Bangladesh foreign minister A H Mahmood Ali has recently said, development of India's northeastern region would benefit Bangladesh equally.

Bangladesh and the northeast share a permanent bond due to their geographical proximity. This bond, which no one can alter, should be made more beneficial for the two. Businessmen on both the sides have already found a great opportunity for mutual benefit that needs to be explored. The development of infrastructure and removal of trade barriers are the challenges which need to be removed. For the northeast, access to Bangladesh's Chittagong port, 75 km from Tripura, and gateway, was of great importance. This has also a direct bearing on India's much talked about "Look East" policy.

The Chief Ministers of India's northeast Tarun Gogoi of Assam, Manik Sarkar of Tripura, Mukul Sangma of Meghalaya and Lal Thanhawla of Mizoram visited Bangladesh along with the then Indian Prime Minister Dr Manmohan Singh a very years ago . The inclusion of the Chief Ministers of the northeast in the prime minister's entourage gave a new dimension, as it had direct ramifications for much desired trade and connectivity that India needs to connect its landlocked States—some 2,62,230 sq. km and about five crore people—through Bangladesh. The political bosses of the northeast laid stress on improving Bangladesh-India relations with the "Seven Sisters" in all sectors and proposed an increase of land ports. They also wanted cooperation in health, education and environment.

"Tripura is a potential hub of trade with Bangladesh in the entire northeast India," the state's Chief Minister Manik Sarkar said. Bangladeshi products have a competitive advantage due to lower transportation costs. Meghalaya Chief Minister Mukul Sangma proposed joint investment with his state giving the "rich deposit of granite and very high quality of limestone". He is of the view that Bangladesh and the northeast have "a lot of potentialities and concerns" and must try to engage in fruitful cooperation. Mr. Gogoi said, "We want connectivity of not only roads and infrastructure…. we want connectivity of minds."

They all praised the resolve of the Sheikh Hasina government to act against India's separatists and insurgents. The government, despite strong political adversaries who often term those insurgents "freedom fighters," has decisively responded to New Delhi's request in this issue. Mr. Tarun Gogoi of Assam thanked Bangladesh for taking steps against the separatist United Liberation Front of Asom (ULFA).

Inaugurating India-Bangladesh conclave in Dhaka recently, Gen VK Singh, who is the last batch of Indian army officers who fought in the Bangladesh Liberation War in 1971, fondly remembers scores of Bangladesh freedom fighters he fought with. He remarked: nothing would move forward "if we do not find mutual benefit".

India, specially its northeast and the east, has great contribution to Bangladesh's emergence as an independent country. Millions of people from East Pakistan, now Bangladesh, took refuge in West Bengal, Assam, Meghalaya and Tripura, when they faced the Pakistani genocidal army, aided by their local Islamist cohorts, in 1971. As a civilian combatant fighter in the historic war, I take the privilege to thank the people of northeast India who gave us all the support we needed during the crucial period.

Paramount Need

The history of the divided subcontinent has been a history of distrust and suspicion. 1971 was an exception, and it lasted only a few years, till 1975 when Bangladesh's founding father Sheikh Mujibur Rahman was assassinated. Therefore, a bold but realistic approach from both sides is expected for the durability of the measures.

There is a paramount need to develop infrastructure rail, road and air connectivity between the Bangladesh and northern states of India, not only for trade and commerce but also for boosting people interaction. For the common good, we all in the region will have to look beyond our geographical boundaries.

The process is on to open Bangladesh's Deputy High Commission in Guwahati and upgrade Agartala Visa Office to an Assistant High Commission to increase diplomatic and commercial presence in the northeast. On the model of the Dhaka-Agartala and Dhaka-Kolkata bus service, recently the direct bus service between Dhaka-Shillong and Dhaka-Guwahati started. There should be direct Dhaka-Guwahati air link. Bangladesh should complement India's endeavour to develop its north-eastern states in her own interest.

Bangladesh has already contributed to northeast's power development by allowing transportation of heavy equipment for Tripura's Palatana Power Plant through its territory. The Tripura government, in return, agreed to supply 100 megawatt of electricity to Bangladesh from Palatana. Once grid connectivity between the two countries is established, it will open up more opportunities for exchange of power.

I am of the strong view that journalists on both sides of the border can play a proactive role to facilitate the bondage in a region which was bedeviled by historic mistrust and prejudices. This, I am confident, would contribute to the region's peace, economic development and stability, and to reduce mistrust and misgivings.

Conclusions

The world has began witnessing a 'new revolution' since the rise of the Internet in the early 1990s. And due to this, new media or what we call the social media have emerged. The positive outcome of this revolution has not only benefited the West, but also the countries in the developing regions like ours.

Many would not perhaps disagree with me that the need for free, independent and responsible media is felt more and more, because threat to the existing media is growingly noticed. Such threats, as I understand, mainly come from the rogue capitalists, vested political groups, organised smugglers' rings and religious extremists having political agenda.

In the countries like ours, the state powers were once the main adversaries of independent journalism. However, they are not the only one in the changed scenario. Powerful corporate capital, unlawful usurpers of power and vested power groups have become equally powerful adversaries of honest journalism.

The social media activists–the bloggers, social site users, mobile phone users, freelance photographers and others, create scopes for social interactions, and promote free thinking. In the mainstream media, however, the practice is different. I would not say that the social media have succeeded replacing the mainstream or virtual media, even after their enormous flourishment. But when the traditional media are reluctant, the social media do not.

However, social media have limitations too.

Bangladesh has a media explosion in the past two decades. The number of daily newspapers is more than a hundred, too large to compare the size and economic conditions! Nonetheless, the mainstream newspapers are free and vibrant. The country has more than 30 television channels, 14 FM and 60 community radios, all in the private sectors. But there are allegations that many of these media outlets are patronized by political or business quarters. Healthy democracy requires healthy and competitive media, but if monopolistic practices by partisan political groups persist, it cannot be seen as a good sign.

The development of the new media is also impressive. Dozens of Internet-based newspapers, journals and periodicals have already made their presence felt. The web newspapers are becoming increasingly popular. And the net editions of all major newspapers are perhaps not less popular than their print editions.

India and Bangladesh, precisely Bangladesh and the India's northeast, must mend fences, and reach out to each other realising the genuine needs of either side. The political leaderships must show prudence to overcome the challenges that have bed-eviled the relations so long by taking quick and appropriate measures. All must realize the fact that geography and history are for India and Bangladesh to be together.

Journalism, whether in peace or in conflict, must demonstrate on its core values; If these values are practiced the profession can be more people-oriented, more human, more constructive and more welfare-oriented.

Media as Facilitators of Peace: Some Requisites

MONALISA CHANGKIJA

Conflict in the Northeast is generally perceived from the prism of insurgency and militancy and worse still, it appears that such conflicts are perceived to exist in a vacuum or in isolation from the various other conflicts that not only create insurgency and militancy but also those that are created by insurgency and militancy. At the outset, I would like to underscore that the commonly believed conflicts created by insurgency and militancy are only a part of the larger conflicts confronting the Northeast, as well as the neighbourhood, and it is these larger conflicts that perhaps pose greater challenges, and spawn greater threats and risks, which the media need to focus on in this region.

Let us appreciate the fact that Northeastern societies were in existence centuries before the rise of some conflicts such as insurgency and militancy. In fact, these are recent developments, not even a century old. Older conflicts relating to histories, ideologies, politics, cultures, traditions, religions, beliefs, superstitions, lore and legends of primarily tribal societies are harder to deal with, especially through and with modern concepts such as democracy and institutions thereof, which are of the alien variety, unmindfully imposed post-Independence on ancient societies with highly developed concepts and practices of democracy, including institutions like the media, which are quite beyond the comprehension of minds that are still psychologically and culturally more attuned to ancient concepts and practices.

Not surprisingly, the media is not generally perceived as an integral institutional component of democracy crucial to nurture and strengthen the democratic ethos to reach higher planes of civilization but perceived more as just another agency that must be viewed with suspicious eyes. The media need to focus on the conflict and challenges thereof, and draw a larger blue print to address these conflicts and challenges to play assertive peace-making roles. Perhaps the primary step is to act as the bridge between the huge communication gap between the media manned by people with totally different and divergent perspectives and its target groups, who have totally different and divergent views of democracy and its institutions, as also of civilization. And this we must appreciate against the background of the two kinds of democracy in operation in this region - our ancient concepts, systems and structures of democracy and the modalities of modern democracy gradually introduced after the arrival of the British.

In the primarily tribal Northeastern region, there are several kinds of power struggles, which are as ancient as Time itself, which the media must be aware of and alive to, and appreciate that they are manifesting in our modern configurations and conflicts in newer avatars. And insurgency and militancy in the Northeast represents some of these power struggles, now of course waged by modern weapons of fire power, which has given a totally new colour to one of these power struggles. So when we talk about conflicts in the Northeast and the need for the media to play a peace-making role and/or facilitate peace in conflict situations, we have to understand and appreciate, and also be able to discern, the numerous kinds of conflicts that exist in our little corner of the world.

The Northeast is normally associated with insurgency and militancy, also now defined as conflict and conflict situations (to be politically correct) but there are conflicts that have been in existence here for centuries hence precede insurgency and militancy movements. That insurgents and militants have sometimes gotten themselves involved in these conflicts and have aggravated conflict situations is another matter. For instance, the Border dispute between Assam and Nagaland ~ land is the main issue of the dispute between the two states. Point 12 of the 16-Point Agreement between the Naga People's Convention and the Government of India in July 1960, under the heading Consolidation of Forests Areas, clearly states:

The delegation wished the following to be placed on record: The Naga delegation discussed the question of the inclusion of the reserve Forests and of contiguous areas inhabited by the Nagas. They were referred to the provisions in Article 3 and 4 of the Constitution, prescribing the procedure for the transfer of areas from one State to another[1].

This bone of contention remains unresolved till today and when there are flare-ups between the people living in the border areas, not only are the Police of the two states engaged, ostensibly to maintain law and order and contain the situation, but even insurgents and militants of the two states inevitably get drawn into these flare-ups. But it would be erroneous to look at and address such situations as conflicts created by insurgency and militancy. It also cannot be denied that a number of border disputes in the Northeast are more the handiworks of over-ground politics than any other force or factor. Moreover, because the Government of India remains indecisive about clear cut borders of the Northeastern states, the disputes fester year by year creating the atmosphere and environment for all kinds of situations to arise, which attract the attention of those who are wont to fish in muddied waters.

While insurgency and militancy have become the most intractable issues that confront the Northeast, let us come back to some other conflicts that have existed before insurgency and militancy gained a larger-than-life notoriety, which is sadly what the Northeast of India is identified with, both by Northeasterners and others from other parts of the country. Some of the other conflicts that are often forgotten and ignored, sometimes even derided, are those that involve issues such as tribalism, perspectives of ethnicity, conflicting aspirations and interests, cultural diversities and dreams and schemes of tribal hegemony, as also power struggles at varied and various levels of society, perhaps due to a multiplicity of value-systems we subscribe to, and we must keep in mind that these are the very same factors that that have also spawned insurgency and militancy. This of course we would be able to understand and appreciate better if we keep in mind the historical fact that not only have tribal societies in the Northeast been rudely tossed from our subsistence economies into modern forms of economies but also the fact that our histories and cultures were unceremoniously hijacked at a certain point of time by alien forces and factors. This has disoriented Northeastern societies and this disorientation has spawned conflicts, which the media in this region cannot ignore if we are to facilitate peace and be peace-makers in conflict situations.

A newer factor that is not only aggravating the existing conflict situations but also creating newer situations of conflict is the new market value-system, culture, systems and demands. These new market value-system, culture, systems and demands are throwing our entire traditional market value-system, culture, systems and demands off balance and our Northeastern societies and communities are caught off-guard and so we are today grappling with an irresistible and an invincible force hitherto unknown to us. Perhaps, this could explain why although the Northeast is unanimous on the issue of the scourge of illegal immigrants, we still remain unsuccessful in abating their onslaught, especially their dominance in the market. This newer market demands cheap labour and maximum profits, which in turn has created another set of conflicts that has turned into an armed one, and allegedly even to the point of being supported, funded and armed by foreign countries.

This newer market also sets off the de-humanization process of human beings across the globe. Now imagine when this process occurs in tribal communities like ours, which have always had a very strong sense and bond of community. Our sense of community is diminishing and our community bonds are weakening because the newer market changes our priorities. Our priorities have already changed beyond recognition and therefore cheap labour for our enterprises is more important that our sense of the collective, more importantly our sense of community and it no longer matters to us who provides that cheap labour. See, this newer market demands and dictates that our individual survival is more important that even patriotism therefore while we publicly posture on the unabated influx of illegal immigrants, privately we hire them because they not only earn us good money but they also save us good money.

Moreover, as our insurgent and militant groups are increasingly entering into the market in the form of taxing businesses and setting up syndicates thereby controlling the market, the influx of illegal immigrants has become a boon for them ~ insurgents and militants have now become partners in controlling our market. Evidently, the newer market has eclipsed the ideological stands of both the people and the insurgents and militants.

Our increased rates of crimes, especially against women and children, must also be perceived from the prism of our changed priorities wherein we prioritize individual survival over collective survival. Let us not forget that perhaps besides religion, nothing is more patriarchal than the market. And the market has always commoditized women and children. So, because we have internalized the inherently patriarchal value-system of particularly the newer market, women and children are viewed as commodities ergo, the increased rates of crimes against women and children.

Clearly, what needs to be underscored here is the fact that standing at the crossroads of the traditional and modernity, Northeastern societies are not very sure as to how to view the media, which is after all, an institution of the modern concept of democracy, and what its agenda is. And when one is not sure of things, one tends to look at them with suspicion, as also treat it as 'unfriendly'. It is from this perception and perspectives, the media here need to draw a blue print to address these multi-faceted issues to facilitate peace in the region, especially keeping in mind that the media too is not only vulnerable to the demands and dictates of the market but in most cases have already succumbed to them unabashedly. So today, instead of focusing on our roles and responsibilities to enlighten our readers and viewers vis-à-vis their right to know, we are more focused on our circulation figures, our advertisement revenue and our TRPs. Today, we are more focused on political patronage rather than highlighting the plights of the disadvantaged and vulnerable sections of our society and the wrong-doings of our law makers.

Against this background, what also needs our attention in the Northeast is an in-depth study of the psychological profiles of our peoples, which have shaped our histories, economies, politics, cultures, traditions, laws, lore and legends, keeping in mind that over the centuries, these very same factors, have also shaped our psychological profiles, as well as the newer market forces and factors, and its dictates and demands, that are reshaping our psychological profiles. The interesting aspect of it all is that the media in the Northeast may be a result of western or modern orientation by way of education and the technological revolution increasingly reaching to and impacting the remotest of areas but the women and men, who make and shape the media in this region, are also products of Northeastern societies and do not escape the influences of the concepts and practices, the cultures and traditions and the entire value-system - old and new - of our Northeastern societies. Here we need to also cannot ignore the threats and risks to the media not only from outside the media but also from within the media, as we are moulded by the soil we grow on, which either positively facilitates or adversely impedes us from facilitating peace in conflict situations.

One kind of impediment towards facilitating peace in conflict situations that the media in the Northeast confront is created by our own fraternity due to our inability or unwillingness to shed our biases and prejudices, as also our traditional and cultural viewpoints of the world in general, or by totally becoming subservient to the value-system and dictates and demands of the newer market. Consequently, we have sidelined one of the tenets of democracy—the role of the facilitator of, as also the platform for freedom of thought and expression to be a real right of our people and also a weapon in our people's hands for their will to be supreme—and unwittingly imprisoned ourselves to the 'dominant' politics, economics, cultures, ideologies, and what is made out to be the 'dominant aspirations' of our peoples, including that of participating in the newer market system. The Northeastern may not have been coerced into this newer market system but it has definitely been lured into it but because the media here has not been as aware as we should have been, we failed to inform and educate our people of the pitfalls of this newer market system and warn them of the consequences. In fact, perhaps the media was the first institution to have surrendered to the newer market system without any resistance.

So then, now the primary challenge for the media in the Northeast is to find ways and means to help our people focus on the numerous issues of conflict and find their own answers and solutions, as also act as a bridge to help our people to find a common platform to address conflicting issues, without abdicating our (the media's) roles and responsibilities clearly underscored as the *raison d'être* for the existence and the necessity of the Fourth Estate in a self-respecting democracy. It is also one of the primary roles of the media to inform, create awareness and educate the people of the predatory nature of the market to which let us not forget, politics is very subservient.

One very sad development that has been taking place in the Northeast in the past couple of decades or so is the culture of ad-hocism that has crept into particularly two most essential aspects of human development—one is education and the other is media. If you pick up any newspaper published in any state of this region, one of the main concerns is the declining quality of education. Besides other factors, compromising the quality of teaching is mainly attributed to this unhappy state of affairs. There is a lot of truth in this because today the teaching profession is perceived as a stop-gap arrangement till one finds a better job with a larger pay packet. This same value is replicated in the media too. Anyone, who can write and speak better than the average person, or has "a saleable TV presence" gives the media a go, while biding her time for a better job. And because it is very difficult to find committed journalists, especially with the proper requisite educational background, print and electronic media houses snap up anyone who shows some enthusiasm. What the media need is not only committed and dedicated personnel but also people who are thoroughly well-versed in history, culture, economics, politics, literature, visual and performing arts and all other subjects related to human existence and survival. To empower ourselves to be facilitators of peace in conflict situations, we need to do more than reporting – of course, in the first place we need to report without bias and prejudice and stick to the facts, avoid assumptions, presumptions, suspicions, veiled allegations and not to give any space for them to read too much between the lines. We need to analyze the situation, explain to our readers and viewers why the situation has arisen in the first place historically, ensure that we do not indulge in any form of rabble-rousing, advise and guide them how to react and respond in such situations, maintain peace – mostly by advising them to curb their tongue and passions, avoid communal references, etc., and maintain our dignity while we do so.

If we look at our television reports today and also some of the Editorials, news reports, columns, features and articles, what comes across clearly is a crisis of dignity. And the crisis of dignity underscores the negation of the media's role as facilitators of peace. In simple words, when we take sides and when we assume the role of the judge and jury, sometimes even that of the executioner, we negate the very essence of the Fourth Estate and reduce ourselves to rabble-rousers and trouble-makers, and in the process we effectively negate not only the impact of the Fourth Estate as well as the significance of the conflict that could have far reaching impact on the political and socio-economic landscape of our land and communities but more imperatively our ability to facilitate peace in conflict situations. In the process, instead of facilitating peace, we facilitate disunity, disharmony more angst, more agony and increase the size of the already existing divides amongst ourselves. It definitely goes without saying that more than any other profession, the Fourth Estate, the media, today needs to be manned by experts in varied and various subjects to do justice to our readers and viewers. The wheels of the Fourth Estate, the media, cannot be oiled by enthusiasm and ad-hocism, and worse still by compromising on the quality of media practitioners. For the Fourth Estate to be effective and efficient, the need of the hour is intellectuals with integrity, not merely people with diplomas and degrees.

Another very lamentable and notable aspect of the media today is arm-chair journalism. While it is not a pretty sight to see electronic media journalists thrusting the mike at the faces of affected people and screaming inane questions at them, it is equally unpalatable to read verbatim the press releases issued by whoever without any background details as to the reasons why a particularly press release was issued and then for the Reporter or the newspaper not to publish later developments on the issue. Photographs and statements of politicians particularly on issues they have no expertise on are not the best of things to wake to in the morning just because a Reporter or Correspondent is a regular member of that politician's entourage. In the first place, journalists aren't supposed to be in the entourage of any politician or public leader or influential person. Maintaining a healthy distance is necessary for objectivity in reporting and informing the people.

It is also very lamentable that today increasingly our Reporters and

Correspondents, as also Editors themselves, are transforming themselves into politicians' publicist and public relations boys and girls. Journalism, public relations and mass communications are very distinct subjects that cannot merge into one as and when convenient. Likewise, today our newspapers and television channels have become the spokespersons of the corporate world. So while there is no space to highlight the plight of widows, battered women, bankrupt farmers, physically and mentally challenged people and the corruption that is increasingly impoverishing our communities, there is no dearth of space for corporate houses to advertise their wares, most of which are not necessary to live a meaningful and productive life.

The potential for the media to facilitate peace in conflict situations are endless however there are forces and factors that limit our potentials and chief amongst them are our own priorities, most of which are not socially sensitive. The media needs to be socially sensitive and sensitized to be able to facilitate peace in conflict situations. This then demands that the media prioritizes its roles and responsibilities and not its agenda. Moreover, this also demands that we do not comprise on the quality of media practitioners. More than any other profession, or vocation, commitment, integrity and expertise are the fundamental requisites of the Fourth Estate for us to be able to bring about change in the profiles of conflict-ridden societies.

Reference

[1] Luingam L and Nandita H., *Nagaland File: A Question of Human Rights*, Lancer International, 1984

Media, Trauma Reporting and Conflict Resolution

PRADIP PHANJOUBAM

The media's role in any conflict situation is not easy as an intellectual proposition, and also dangerous as a physical responsibility. There are simply too many compromises forced on the media worker, so much so that the job often is reduced to just a tight rope walk, keeping a balance not so much out of any sense of objectivity, but to save one's skin.

The biggest and the most awesome confinements are the demands of the conflicting nations and nationhood. The establishment and its challengers, both demand loyalty to their conception of nationhood and expect the media, as also the rest of the citizenry, to not question their fundamentals, on the pain of extreme penalties. Both perceive the violence they perpetrate as legitimate from their own perspective, and it is amidst such a war that the media in an insurgency situation is caught in.

But the dividing lines of the conflicting notions of nationhood are much more complex and nuanced. Hence the extremely violent confrontations between ethnic groups over homelands, particularly so because physically these homelands overlap, most often, totally. Apart from the danger of becoming victims of violence, the intriguing question is also one of defining what constitutes objectivity in reporting these conflicting visions. A good way to begin may be to scrutinize what we generally consider without questioning as legitimate.

A distinction must also have to be made between the provincial media, and the mainstream, metropolitan media. Their dynamics as well as resources are a world apart. As for instance, most of the media organisations in Manipur are journalist owned, and basically cottage industries by comparison with their metropolitan counterparts. Hence, often their values and commitments cannot be fairly assessed by the same yardstick. My opinion is, although far poorer, the provincial media's commitment to social issues is much more, and this is so because their perspectives is more inclined towards that of the subjects of the social phenomena than distanced, disinterested objective observers of the same events. This has its advantages as well as disadvantages. I will briefly touch on this issue too in this paper.

Defining Legitimacy

It is time for the human rights debate in Manipur, where the endless string of mayhem for the past many decades has disoriented the people form the finer points of rights and entitlements, is given a fresh approach. The clash between draconian laws and brutal counter laws of decrees and diktats, has desensitized the finer appreciations of the beauty of even the much hyped idea of freedom. Today, if an ordinary man on the street were to be posed the question as to what he thinks freedom is, the answer in all likelihood would be the rote, superficial, textbook or else indoctrinated definition of it. If he or she understands or believes more than just what it is being advocated to mean, the answer is likely to be a studied silence.

A silence induced by fear, whichever side of the fence the belief leans towards amidst the intense conflict over the issue in the place. But an honest answer to the question is important. For one thing, on it will hinge the solution to many of our problems. For another, many other questions of import will necessarily have to be derivatives of it. As for instance, linked to it would be our understandings of rights, justice and a sense of a benign republican polity.

When things get complicated, it is always helpful to refer to the thumb-rule that says begin from the basic. Economics Nobel Laureate Amartya Sen says in his book *Development as Freedom*, proposed the examination of "unfreedoms" to understand the status of the more ethereal "freedom". What are the conditions in our individual as well as community life that shackle and weigh down our ability to live with dignity? Poverty, unemployment, deprivation of political voice, inadequate empowerment to participate and formulate policies that govern our lives, depletion of a sense of purpose in life, shrinking of hope of acquiring the skills and abilities to enhance one's quality of life? What are the "unfreedoms" that are coming in the way of our sense of a more comprehensive "freedom"? We will not presume to know the answer but all we can say is that these are material for honest and intense introspection for all of us at this juncture of our history. This is also the only way we can separate the illusory from the substantial, so vital in our situation.

More urgently, a similar introspective approach is also called for to refresh our understanding of the "human rights" question. The question as to what is "just" and what is "right", may be relatively easy to answer from the legal standpoint but not so when it is considered as a moral query. Two events in Imphal in the past few months portrayed this difficulty convincingly. One was a play by theatre director, Ratan Thiyam, called "*Kurukshetragi Pirang*" (The Tears of Kurukshetra) which looked beyond the text of the *Mahabharata* and considered what might have happened after the great war. It was supposed to be a virtuous war that the five *Pandava* brothers fought against their 100 *Kourava* cousins and this war left not only the "non-virtuous" 100 dead but devastated the entire country, leaving only war widows and orphans to wail and mourn their dead. If a virtuous war results in such devastation, what meaning does virtue make anymore, is the question delivered with such a visual punch characteristic of the director's style.

The other event was a series of two lectures by Charles Douglas Lummis, organized by the my newspaper, *Imphal Free Press* and Manipur Research Forum, in Imphal. In one of these lectures, he invoked Max Weber's idea of the claim of the "State" to monopoly over "legitimate violence" and "right to belligerency" distinguishing it from any other organization, political or otherwise. The assumption here is, only the State has a right to exercise "legitimate violence" and to "declare war". The non-state players in our conflict situation also presume these rights, aspiring as they do to be States. In the Weberian sense then, they are very much the two side of the same coin. The point that Lummis made however is, whatever the legitimacy of the State's claim, in the 20th century alone, "legitimate violence" and the "right to belligerency" left 200 million dead (estimate done by Hawaii University). Can "legitimate violence" then still be morally legitimate? The lesson is very much the same as Thiyam's play communicated. They both demonstrate that this space between the legal and moral is where we must attempt to relocate our debates on rights and freedom. This yardstick can be extremely useful in our own assessment of our own actions. For indeed, while the obsession has been with the legality of action, few have ever moderate this vision with the moral question. The means as well as the end must have to be subjected to this oral interrogation.

Honest Media

Not as opposed to a free media, but in addition to being a free media, what is also extremely important is giving substance to the idea of an honest media. Of course we are aware we skate on very thin ice, by necessity, when we even place a foot in the realm of the abstract. "Honesty" for instance is heavily nuanced, as the stage explorations of Norwegian dramatist Henrik Ibsen touchingly and convincingly bring out. For indeed, the untruth of the white lie may in this sense be actually noble, and in a spiritual way, show a fidelity not to hard facts but to a realm beyond. So very often, honesty and dishonesty are not so obvious, but are deeply buried below multiple nuances of a complex subject. Sincere introspections and discourses must have to be about digging out these nuances and then reassessing our situations with them as the backdrop. It is also against this backdrop that our sense of right and wrong, or call it conscience if you will, must be placed.

But the problem is, when your house is on fire, there is hardly any likelihood that you will have time to think of anything else but the fire. And so, the chief concern of the Manipur media today is media freedom from external pressures. There is hardly the leisure as yet to think beyond this and to begin touching the nuances of abstract but essential subjects as honesty etc. Much like what Prof. Lummis, implied of the question of rule of law. Things are so chaotically bad in Manipur today that just the return of the rule of law can do it wonders as a first step. But this first step can hardly be the last, for the rule of law too can become extremely oppressive. As for instance, to take an example which nobody in Manipur would miss, the Armed Forces Special Powers Act (AFSPA) is an instrument of the rule of law. Hence, in any consideration of rightness and wrongness, there is the need ultimately to realize there is something beyond even the rule of law. The rule of law ultimately has to be built on the foundation of certain innate and universal qualities of the individual, such as "the innate resistance in a man to kill another man", in Prof. Lummis' own words. "Radical citizenship" and "radical democracy" would then be for the civil society to provide the foil to ensure the rule of law does not stray from these universal qualities.

The Manipur media too must then first ensure that its basic editorial freedoms are guaranteed. It must continue to resist and challenge all oppressive pressures to control its editorial discretions, be it from the underground establishment or from the government authorities. It must also be brave enough to acknowledge that while there is a tendency over the years for the government to relax its controls, sometimes to the extent of promoting anarchy, it is the diktats from underground organizations and their fronts, which have been the source of most media fetters. This too, we must add, is easing up. Once these overt threats are overcome, it must begin the soul search for the nuances of the qualities that concern us most, and which we have always taken so much for granted. These would include, as we have briefly touched upon earlier, honesty, but also freedom for instance. For beyond freedom from physical threats to personal wellbeing, this concept too is extremely nuanced. As a footnote it must be said, in digging out these nuances, there can be no medium better than the arts, as men like Ibsen have demonstrated. Who says the arts have ceased to be relevant to modern life no more than their ornamental value?

Understanding Insurgency

The problem of insurgency or peace has never been, and can never be in black and white terms, as many have made it out to be. It is definitely not as simple as the President George Bush's, defining line between friends and foes, in his nation's war on terrorism, that "you are either with us or against us." This, we suppose, is the kind of mindset that has thrown up theories like the "Clash of Civilizations" and made them acceptable widely. Never mind the existence of counter theories of civilization as basically the epitome of the expansive and accommodative aspect of the human spirit. The statement is interesting in the context of this seminar as well, for this very often is also the trap the militaristic approach to counter insurgency falls into.

While in an armed insurgency situation, it would be naïve not to expect an armed retaliation from the establishment, this retaliation has to be necessarily accompanied by a longer political vision of peace that takes care of issues rather than insurgent firepower. The problem often is one of an acute limitation of vision that fails to inform that things are not as simple as an objective type examination question paper where the answer is merely either a true or a false. Contrary to this, in any human problem, insurgency situations included, between the black and the white; between the friend and the foe; between those who are "with us" and those who are not; there is a whole spectrum of colours and nuances of support and sympathy and indifference, and many of these sentiments and beliefs literally overlap. It is a fact that not all of the many who are not "with us," are not necessarily "against us," and equally, many who are "with us" may not be working in our best interest even if unintentionally. Incompetence, insensitivity, corruption, political myopia on the part of those in charge of the establishment and in command of its resources, are at the root of many of our ills.

Hence, the need to identify these nuances, or else at least acknowledge the existence of the spectrum of colours and shades between the two poles of "with us" and "against us" in looking for a resolution to social conflicts. Conflict resolution cannot be all about eliminating and exterminating all opposition, or of reducing the choices in negotiating this problem to the two mutually exclusive sets of rights and wrongs. On the contrary, it must consist of labouring to bring everybody to see the reality before them and then to project a future with this understanding as the foundation.

To be a little more specific, insurgency in the northeast, has been very much a product, if not an outgrowth of the historical, economic and political circumstances of the society. It is the manifestation of unarticulated furies within the society and indeed Frantz Fanon's description of such insurrections as the "mailed fist" of a people with a sense of impotence at articulating the anger within, is apt. There is hence, even at points when the brutalities of insurgency have alienated it considerably from the ordinary men and women, and even when it has become evident that insurgency is headed towards a dead end, there is always an unseen, even if distant, umbilical cord that preserves a fraternal feeling among those who have chosen the path of rebellion and the people by and large amongst whom they operate.

Hence, even those who now believe the causes of insurgency have lost its relevance on account of numerous shifts in the paradigms that define and give value to these causes, will recommend a political solution in which the prodigals are guaranteed a legitimate place in the society, rather than the domineering extermination theory that has among others, made even the United Nations arguably "irrelevant," split Europe into Old Europe and New Europe, and left a larger part of the world with a helpless sense of moral indignation. This seeming soft vision of insurgency does not however mean the society has cut its other umbilical cords, particularly the one with the establishment.

As for instance, no matter how much tough action by the security forces is resented, there are traffic jams outside the Kangla in Imphal, (the old seat of power of the erstwhile kingdom of Manipur, now garrisoned and occupied by the Indian Army) everytime there is a call for recruitment rally by any unit of the security forces, on account of young men scrambling for a chance to take part. It should be evident from this and many other similar examples that nothing indeed is in black and white when dealing with such issues. In such a scenario, the job before the media has never been easy. On the one hand it has to come to terms with the immediate law and order fallouts, which include covert and sometimes overt intimidation from various underground organizations to forgo the right to edit or criticize. On the other, despite these infringements, the need still is to tread carefully so as not to end up being blind to the finer undercurrents and dynamics of the society which drive insurgency.

There is also the other danger of the establishment coming down on the media if it is seen to have overstepped into the wrong side of the law in walking this fine balance. Examples of the misfortune of media-men and media organizations on this count too are many. It is indeed a tightrope walk for the media operating in this scenario. The fact that in the past few years, at least five journalists have even lost their lives and many more suffered harassment from either side of the conflict, should give an idea of the occupational hazard in this extraordinary situation.

Much of the problems in the northeast have been also among others, one of an inability to strike a balance between the subjective and the objective visions of the changing world and the inadequacy of the responses to the ever emerging and renewing reality. The two visions, rather than complement each other, have instead been treated and pushed separately, too often at the neglect of the other. Because the two are treated as mutually exclusive, no serious attempt has been made to build a bridge between them. The broad theme of this paper is to propose that a convergence is needed, for the problem at hand is at the same time subjective and objective.

Subjective aspirations give a community the sense of purpose that no worldly incentives can buy, and without this sense of purpose, the basic integrity of the society can fall apart. It may very well be that the high incidences of AIDS, drugs, promiscuity and general rootlessness amongst the so called elite section of the youth of the region, is directly correlated to this destruction, or at least degeneration, of their subjective worlds. It may be noted Manipur and Nagaland are amongst the ten states in India to have seen the highest percentage population occurrences of AIDS. Other northeasten states, including Mizoram, are only marginally better off. Modernity can go awry in the event of the inability of the inner and the outer worlds of a community to moderate each other.

The subjective world view represented by the mushrooming demands for ethnic exclusive rights, hence must negotiate with the viewpoint which sees the problems of the northeast as fundamentally one of a lack of development and modernity. Unfortunately both have come to occupy the opposite poles of the same issue. The challenge then, to a great extent is to evolve structures where the two can be simultaneously addressed and moderated.

Subject or Object

Much of the problems in the Northeast have been also among others, one of an inability to strike a balance between the subjective and the objective visions of the changing world and the inadequacy of the responses to the ever emerging and renewing reality. The two visions, rather than complement each other, have instead been treated and pushed separately, too often at the neglect of the other.

The Problem as a Subject

A personal experience will illustrate the first proposition of the vulnerability of the subjective vision as a stand alone explanation of the northeast problem. In many ways the major onus of correction of this aberration of vision will have to rest on the ethnic communities whose worlds are today on the verge of being shattered by the irreconcilability of their own vision with the world outside.

Towards the end of 2004, I had done a series of three articles after a trip to Italy. One of them was about how wonder-struck, I was at my first encounter with wireless internet at the Vienna airport. Barely two years after in 2006, I re-read what I wrote, and to my amazement found it silly. The wi-fi as the technology is known, is practically everywhere, even in northeast India. The pace of wireless telephony development has been, to say the least, breakneck. Today, it is not just wi-fi but a lot more. The subject is no longer a matter of mystery, but very much an everyday reality for even those of us in remote Manipur.

If the same article were to be written now, rather than hope for any appreciation from readers anywhere, it would only attract mocking laughters. In the two years that have gone by, so much of the contextual background has changed, and the context is what gives meaning to any text. One is also reminded of the classic real life story of the Japanese soldier who got lost in the jungles of the Philippines during the heat of the World War II, and emerged from his hiding 30 years later in the mid 1970s, thinking Japan was still at war with America. The contrast between a subjective world and a changed objective reality could not have been more stark than the dilemma that presented itself to the unfortunate soldier at the time he was found.

The lesson is, since the context is not a static phenomenon, there is a need for even script writers of ideologies and ideological wars, to reassess their thought processes continually against the ever changing contexts. Inability to do this would, like the wi-fi story, make the ideas themselves redundant, obsolete, and even silly. Such a predicament is today not altogether remote. For far too often, in the northeast region, today's wars are being fought on yesterday's slogans.

The issues for instance of "homeland", "ethnic identity", "tradition" or for that matter the struggles for sovereignty from a "colonizing" nation etc., will have to be reassessed against this understanding. Picking up just the last point, for all that matters, the "colonizing" nation against which the struggles for freedom were launched in the first place, may not be the same nation any longer, so that the struggles themselves stand the risk of becoming out of sync.

The inward looking definition of identity and ethnicity has other dangers. When a certain identity is made to hang on symbols that have become redundant, the identity itself would sooner than later become redundant too. Perhaps the inadequacy of the answers to these questions is behind the endemic and viciously circuitous nature of many of the conflict situations that have afflicted the region.

The Problem as Objects

One the other hand is the interpretation that the problem of northeast is one that can be objectively enumerated, and consequently objectified remedies prescribed. The formula is encapsulated in the classic approach to counter-insurgency in a "carrot and stick" policy frame. Subdue insurgency militarily and at the same time pour in money to accelerate "development". Six decades after insurrections first reared their heads in the northeast, neither the carrot nor the stick has managed to do what they were supposed to do.

The failure of the carrot and stick approach cannot have been more pronounced than in Manipur. In September 2006, during a session of the Manipur Assembly, chief minister' Okram Ibobi Singh's made a clarification on the floor of the Assembly that in the 16 years the state government introduced a surrender policy for insurgents, only 377 underground activists from 19 different organizations actually bit the bait. This makes for a pathetic story, to say the least. If one were to average it out, it translates into a little less than 20 persons per organization in the 16 years, or, a little over one person in a year per organization. Considering a bulk of the surrenders would have been from the numerous vague, seldom heard of organizations, surrenders from the organizations that really count, would practically be nil. So much for a surrender policy. A lot many more policy framers and executives would have retired or else died of old age in the 16 years that have gone by.

But what is even more surprising is, even the few who have surrendered have not been given what they were promised as part of the policy.

Failing a final settlement of the issues that spawned insurgency in the first place, it is always reasonable to be skeptical about the prospect of success of any surrender policy. This is true even in states where massive surrenders is said to have happened, as was the case in Assam.

In the 1990s, during the height of counter insurgency operations against the United Liberation Front of Asom, ULFA, code named "Operation Bajrang", massive well-publicized surrender ceremonies were organized by both the state police as well as the Army. In one such ceremony, more than 1500 ULFA cadres were said to have laid down arms to the Army. The pictures of those arms however raised many eyebrows in the media as well as in other circles.

But even if the benefit of the doubt were to be the privilege of the surrender authorities, the question that cannot escape scrutiny is, have these surrenders made any difference to insurgency in the state as such. For if the surrenders were anything to go by, the ULFA would have been nothing more than the debris of its former self by now. This is exactly what is not the case and today the same authorities are having to court the same underground organization for a negotiated settlement. Is this an undeclared official acknowledgement that all the much vaunted surrender ceremonies had no more value than the drama they were taken for?

The Manipur case is perhaps the hardest proof that solution to insurgency is not just about the classic official line of "carrot and stick" policy. Regardless of the truth in the "criminalization and lumpenization" of insurgency in recent times, insurgency is still not a simple matter. The flimsiness of a total equation between insurgency and unemployment was also thoroughly exposed. It may very well be that unemployment is a big factor behind insurgency, but the issue definitely goes much deeper. Youth frustration and unemployment, in this sense, must be finding a bigger outlets in drugs and other socially deviant behaviours, than insurgency.

Hence a rehabilitation policy would work better for the former category of manifestation of youth frustration, but not the latter, for the latter is also something else besides youth frustration. Exploring that something else is what would provide the magic key to unravel the problem. Unfortunately, not too many who have the power to make the difference have been bothered or resourceful enough to apply their minds to the space where that something else is located.

Transforming Conflict

Transforming conflict to a condition of peace is not simple. The Manipur government's surrender policy has proven this. That there have not been enough surrenders is itself a failure, but equally, the government's inability to find a way to rehabilitate the relatively few who have surrendered meaningfully, is a pointer to the complexity of the issue. In a hypothetical situation where the various insurrections in the region have buried their hostilities with the government, this problem would still remain and quite possibly even compound.

The question would be, what do you do with thousands of young men and women who had given up the best part of their youth pursuing, rightly or wrongly, a nationalistic ideal that involved waging war against the larger nation, into which they would now to be accommodated? Shouldn't state governments in the northeast as well as the Union, begin thinking in terms of investing some time, energy and capital, into a quest for such answers? After the Manipur's surrender policy fiasco, this need should have become at least a little more urgent.

From the Manipur government's surrender policy experience, as well as that of the ongoing "peace" parleys between the NSCN (both factions: NSCN-IM and NSCN-K) and government of India, one or two other things are clear. The unsaid but universal thing about an insurgency situation is that there are always much more than meets the eye behind its dynamics. Its contributory causes are many, including inconsistencies in history, economic structures, development, identity alienation etc. It is also very much related to administrative weaknesses and incompetence, but above all, official corruption that continually trample upon all senses of fair play and justice.

The initial reaction of societies exposed to such conditions is one of awe and submission amongst the larger masses, and a general cynicism amongst the intelligentsia and elite, dictated by the sense that if you cannot beat the system, join it. But the social mechanism is not a dead phenomenon, in thought or action. It is organically conditioned to transform itself to respond to any stimulus fittingly. Under a condition of constant and consistent abuse, it mutates and its reaction can become extraordinary, in extremity and cruelty. To a good extent insurgency is also about such a transformation. Within a matter of a few years, moderate societies have become blood thirsty. Insurgency in this way, is a price the society pays for its neglect and insensitivities of the past.

Managing conflict then, it may turn out, is simpler than formulating a transition of conflict into a condition of peace. While it is true thoughts of the bridge would become relevant when the river is reached, but it it is the duty of any government to anticipate future needs. An abject lack of such vision has been far too often the stumbling block of the Manipur leadership. If it was otherwise, the surrender policy it introduced in 1990, (possibly out of a political whim aimed at hogging limelight rather than result) would not have been such a miserable flop.

Politics of Development

That insurgency cannot have solely a military solution is widely acknowledged, even though there are still die-hard believers, but it is the proposition that development is not everything which needs a little more elaboration. The first question that comes to mind in tackling a subject as complex as development is, can there be an empirical method to measure it? Very often, the tendency has been to equate development with growth absolutely, but can this be justified? A lot many economists do believe this can be, and others don't. Economics being at its very basic, the study of human behaviour and aspiration, perhaps there is an inevitability of a touch of the latter "philosophical approach" which believes that while income and growth are essential components of development, they can be by no means all of there is about the problem.

The argument is, there are certain other factors that make development holistic and complete, and this is as Amartya Sen puts it in his book *Development as Freedom*. Sen calls these "freedoms", and proceeds to calibrate their quality through "unfreedoms". The less "unfreedoms" there are the more "freedoms".

In this approach the popular indices of development such as gross domestic product, GDP, and income, are important to the extent that they create the condition for freeing people from "unfreedoms" to live life as they would by providing the fuel for actualizing their individual aspirations and imagination. The example that Sen uses to demonstrate this argument is interesting. It is a known fact that by and large African Americans have lower incomes than White Americans, but their incomes, although lower in comparison to their White countrymen, is significantly higher than people in most Third World countries even after taking into account the differences in the costs of living etc. Yet, statistics say that African Americans have a much lower life expectancy than the denizens of most countries in the Third World. The deduction is, quality of life is not always a direct derivative of GDP or income. This is exactly where the "philosophical economists" see a problem area in conceptualizing the whole notion of development.

It is again precisely because there exists such a problem area that the agenda of development has been prone to politicization. People in the northeast are all too familiar as to what this means. In fact the place's understanding of development has been grotesquely skewed to mean only externally delivered economic packages which can be translated through various backdoor means and leakages, at the soonest possible into hard cash, expending the least energy. Corruption is the immediate manifestation. The politics of development has also been a very convenient handle for the carrot and stick policy makers. This sordid drama is today a part of life of the northeast people, and true development remains the casualty. The economic bails are necessary but these must actually be "bails" to kick start a process that will liberate the people from the binds of poverty, unemployment, a sense of deprivation resulting from a lack of appropriate skills and education, ill health, malnutrition etc, and not merely counter insurgency measures.

This "philosophical" approach to developmental economic thinking is in many ways an emphasis on the need for the objectification of the subjective visions of the victims. In the end it is a matter of identifying what constitutes quality of life of the people under scrutiny that matter the most. Consequently, it is also the quality and intent, rather than just the size of economic bails that should impress.

Media's Role in Enforcing Change in Northeast

SAMIR K PURKAYASTHA

Media in India's Northeast is trapped in myriads of conflicts that have been sweeping the region for about seven decades. Confronting parties involved in these conflicts have often tried to suppress news or gain control over the media space through manipulation, allurement and, most importantly, intimidation.

The first instance of State manipulation to suppress news to quell an uprising in the region was witnessed even before India had attained freedom. A day before India's tryst with destiny, the Naga National Council (NNC), the omnipotent political platform of the Nagas in those days, declared Naga National Independence. But the outside world did not get to know about the defiance of the Nagas as the NNC's telegram addressed to leading newspapers of the country, informing about its proclamation of independence, was not despatched by the post master of the Kohima post office following an instruction from the then deputy commissioner of the Naga Hills, Charles Pawsey[1].

In the initial days of insurgency in the Northeast, the absence of a strong media in the conflict zones had given the Indian state a free run to commit gross excesses in the name of counter-insurgency operation, particularly in Nagaland and Mizoram. It is a matter of serious debate whether a democrat like Jawaharlal Nehru would have ordered a full-scale army operation and imposition of an undemocratic law like Armed Forces (Special Powers) Act 1958 in Nagaland had there been a strong media to keep a tab on the transgression of basic rights of its own citizens by the State.

During my long stint as journalist in the Northeast, I came across countless people in Nagaland and Mizoram who had to bear the brunt of army highhandedness during the 1950s and 1960s. Their villages were burnt, uprooted and clustered as part of the infamous "grouping" policy adopted by the security forces in a bid to isolate the insurgents from their sympathisers. There were also widespread allegations of torture and rape.

But while scouring media archives, I hardly came across any elaborate write-ups and articles published in the national media those days depicting the horrific acts. This proves media's indifference to the country's peripheral region during those formative days.

Narratives about this troubled region in whatever little coverage the national media or the few regional newspapers published from Shillong and Guwahati gave had a colonial hangover. The image of the tribal people inhabiting the hilly regions beyond the plains of the Brahmaputra had been portrayed to the so-called mainlanders as either savage, barbarian, naked head hunters or gun-wielding troublemakers who loved to kill any outsider at the drop of a tree leaf in their jungle habitations. So, when my father decided to take up a job in the Naga Hills in the early 1960s, my grandfather apparently got the shock of his life.

Olympian Talimeran Ao, who spent most of those turbulent days in Calcutta (now Kolkata) as a Mohun Bagan footballer, in an interview with me at his Golaghat Road residence in Dimapur in 1995, had recollected how people were mystified to find him completely different from the image of a Naga they had come to accept. He was a soft-spoken and a jovial medical student, whereas a popular perception about Nagas, thanks to colonial narratives, was that of ferocious head-hunters or ragtag guerrillas pursing a utopian ideology.

It was again due to the absence of a strong independent media in the troubled region that the nation was mostly left unaware of the fact that the Hunter and Toofani jet fighters of the Indian Air Force had strafed and dropped hundreds of incendiary bombs on Aijal, now Aizawl, (the then district headquarters of Lushai Hills, a district in Assam) on March 5 and 6, 1966, reducing houses, schools, markets, churches and even hospitals to ashes.

In the aftermath of the unprecedented air raids, the government of Assam sent two MLAs, Stanley DD Nichols Roy and Hoover H Hynniewta, both from Assam's erstwhile Khasi Hills district, and Lok Sabha MP from Shillong GG Swell on a fact-finding mission to Aizawl on March 30. Later in April, Nichols Roy moved a motion in the Assam House castigating the air attack. His motion is now part of the Assam Assembly proceedings.

But as there was no reporting from ground zero, one of the most shameful chapters of independent India remained largely in the domain of speculation with the Indian government stoutly denying any such action. The then Prime Minister Indira Gandhi in a statement published in the *Hindusthan Standard* on March 9, 1966, claimed that the air force was merely "deployed to drop men and supplies."

Mizo historian JV Hluna in his book *Debates on Mizo Problems on Insurgencies, with Special Reference to the Contributions of Stanley DD Nichols Roy, MLA, and Hoover H Hynniewta, MLA,* pointed out that the only sources of information regarding the insurgency in Mizoram for the outside world those days were the words of the Assam chief minister, the Assam chief secretary and the prime minister.

Presentation of selective news, sourced from government officials and ministers, to rest of India created a very negative impression about the people of the region for the rest of the country. This prejudice still prevails as has been often manifested in the racial attacks on northeast people in the metropolises.

On the other hand, the apathy of the Indian national media and a large section of intelligentsia toward the sufferings of the people of this frontier region sowed the seed of antagonism among the natives toward the so called mainlanders. As a result, the 'local-outsider' divide festered.

The mistrust and schism still persist, though over the years, interaction and mingling of people from the Northeast and rest of India have increased. Media coverage about the region, too, has increased and more importantly narratives and perspectives are also changing. It was heartening to see the outrage in the national media--which once was caught napping when Naga villages were burnt and Aizawl was bombed in the 50s and 60s--- over the brutal killing of a student from Arunachal Pradesh Nido Tania in the nation's capital early this year.

In fact, things started to change since the 70s when the government of India realised the futility of its one-dimensional crackdown policy. It then started making some concessions to fulfil the aspirations of various ethnic groups. As a result of which several new states and union territories were created. Central funds were generously pumped in to sustain them. Along with central funds came a group of contractors and suppliers. And they in turn brought work forces from outside to the region. The troubled zone of the region was no longer a *terra incognita*, rather, for many unscrupulous businessmen it became a treasure trove.

As the stakes of mainland states started growing in the Northeast, national media also started showing interest in the development of the region. Many reputed newspapers and news agencies began deploying their correspondents in the capitals of these nascent states. Creation of new states also created scope for income for local newspapers as state government advertisements were forthcoming to sustain them.

It is worth noticing the correlation between formation of autonomous councils and establishment of new newspapers in the headquarters of these autonomous district councils such as Diphu, Haflong and Kokrajhar. This underscores the role of government advertisement in the rise of local newspapers.

According to the Registrar of Newspapers for India (RNI), there are 803 registered newspapers in Assam today. Arunachal Pradesh has 23, Manipur 219, Meghalaya 69, Mizoram 186, Nagaland 22 and Tripura has 140 registered newspapers and journals. Of course many of these exist only in the RNI list, while some others publish a few copies only to circulate among the concerned departments and offices on those dates when there are government advertisements.

Apart from the local newspapers, the Kolkata-headquartered *The Telegraph* has two editions, in Guwahati and Jorhat, and *The Times of India* has one in Guwahati. Of late the region, particularly Assam, has also witnessed mushrooming of television channels.

Impact of Media Proliferation

Proliferation of local media has played a significant role in challenging the stereotype and discrimination to a large extent. India no longer ends in Kolkata. It has definitely encompassed Guwahati, if not Itanagar, already.

There is a genuine urge for course correction among at least a section of policy makers. More importantly, unlike in the past, as was evident in Indira Gandhi's statement to *Hindusthan Standard* about the Aijawl bombing, the Central government is no longer in a denial mode about the apathy faced by the region.

Creation of the Department for Development of North Eastern Region (DoNER) and charting of Look East Policy are some indications of New Delhi's policy reorientation toward the region. The Northeast is no longer viewed as a periphery of the country, but as an all important link between world's two biggest markets. Growing numbers of domestic tourist to the region is also an indicator of the changing mindset of the people from the mainland towards the region.

As per the Economic Survey of Ministry of Finance 2011-12, the highest growth rates of the services sector were in the north-eastern states of Arunachal Pradesh (34.9 per cent) and Sikkim (30.1 per cent). Another northeast state Mizoram also recorded higher than national average growth in the sector. Peace that has prevailed in these states has contributed to the growth.

According to statistics provided by the DoNER ministry in 2011, the per capita income in five northeastern states has increased substantially with Arunachal Pradesh, Mizoram and Sikkim bettering the national average[2].

According to DoNER, the total plan investment by the centre to northeastern states in the Tenth Five Year Plan (that is from 2002-07) was a staggering 80,000 crore rupees. In 2006-07, the per capita central assistance for state plan for northeastern states was 2,241 rupees compared to 570 rupees for the non-special category states. As this funding pattern continues, northeastern states are receiving highest per capita level of central assistance among states in India[3].

To bridge the cultural divide, Arunachal Pradesh Chief Minister Nabam Tuki on February 18, 2014 told journalists in Delhi that the Central government had agreed to include geography, history and tradition and culture of the indigenous people of the northeastern states in NCERT textbooks[4].

Of course, there is still a long way to go for a holistic transformation. But, as they say, diagnosis is the first step to cure. Today the country is well aware of the issues confronting the region and these issues—be it the need to scrap Armed Forces (Special Powers) Act or discrimination against people from Northeast in the metros or need for special assistance for the region (to mention a few)—are widely debated in the national media.

The local media can certainly take credit for this turnaround. If today Irom Chanu Sharmila is almost a household name in India or the AFSPA debate is ramped up by many decibels in the corridors of power, it is because of the persistent campaign by the media in Manipur. Similarly, Nagaland media can also take some credit for the then prime minister Atal Bihari Vajpayee's recognition of the "uniqueness of Naga history" in 2003. Indeed, media in the Northeast have persistently highlighted issues of discrimination, neglect and rights violations and also succeeded in forcing a narrative as well as policy shift.

But this is just one part of the story. On the flip side, the zeal and persistency shown by the media in covering the region's victimisation, as well as in mobilising mass opinion against it, are absent when it comes to the need for highlighting the internal deficiencies that are also hugely contributing to the region's underdevelopment.

For instance, despite corruption being a major hindrance to the region's growth, there is no persistent campaign or attempt to mobilise public opinion against the menace. How many protest rallies have we seen against corruption in the region, which is otherwise known for agitation, blockades and bandhs? How many editorials or opinion pieces were written on the subject? The answer is very few.

A survey which revealed 87 per cent Indians outside the Northeast could not name the seven sisters commanded a lot of attention and media space in the region two years ago. The finding has been projected as damming evidence of the nation's apathy towards the region. But have we ever tried to find out how many of us in the northeast know how much about the region? How many persons in Agartala or Aizawl can tell how many districts are there in Nagaland?

How many cases of reverse discrimination so-called outsiders face in the Northeast are highlighted in the media? Last year, three businesspersons were attacked and set on fire within a span of a few days. All three later succumbed to their injuries. But there was hardly any media outrage in the region over these incidents.

The reverse discrimination the so-called outsiders faced in the region was aptly summed up by Patricia Mukhim in an article in the Hindu:

In Meghalaya, in the late 1970s, the Khasi Students' Union — a body that is anything but student-like and has in its fold members who have either dropped out of school or are too long in the tooth to be considered students — launched an insidious attack on the Bengalis living in Shillong. Their reason for doing so is simplistic — the non-tribals are responsible for all the ills that afflict Khasi society. So attractive was the slogan "Khasi by birth, Indian by accident" that the words were splattered across public walls in the city. Claiming to be the vanguard of Khasi society, the KSU then went on a rampage, pulling non-tribals out of buses and lynching them. A pregnant woman, Gouri Dey, was lynched in public but no one was nabbed and the case died a natural death since no one would give evidence. The next phase of communal violence saw a new set of victims — the Nepali settlers who have also lived in the State since it was a part of Assam, and the Biharis who kept cows and supplied milk to the residents. Another time, a number of Bihari families were burnt alive in the dead of night. The culprits were never caught and no one has been indicted in any of the acts of communal carnage that happened in Meghalaya[5].

It is high time the media starts playing a more proactive role in exposing the internal threats and the self-styled vanguards of society who are perhaps doing more harm to the region than good.

Of course, it is easier said than done, given the constraints under which the media performs in the region. Blaming the media for failing to expose the internal deficiencies will be like shooting the messenger.

With the proliferation of local media, the tables have turned. Kh Kabi after analysing the contents of two newspapers, *The Nagaland Post* and *The Telegraph*, pointed out in his book *Naga Peace Process and Media* that both these newspapers sourced their story on Naga peace process mostly from NSCN. Nagaland Post sourced 45.2 per cent story on the issue from NSCN, while in case of *The Telegraph* it is 49.1 per cent.

It is no longer the State, but the non-state actors who are ruling the roost in the media space. The intrigue applied by the State to suppress news has now been replaced by intimidation by these non-state actors. Media persons are under constant pressure to toe the lines of militant groups, who often even force the media to shape public opinion to their advantage. It is they who dictate how they be projected by the media. Their press releases and statements are forced to be published verbatim.

According to Asian Human Rights Commission, harassment of media persons in the form of killings, bombings, threat to life and property, assaults, and arrests has become common as now both state and non-state actors try to generate and control the flow of (mis)information in the region.

Since 1991, in the state of Assam alone, 26 journalists had been killed by militant outfits, the timber mafia, criminal gangs, and 'unidentified killers'. However, no single person has been brought to book for these crimes.

In July 2012 Tongam Rina, an associate editor with *The Arunachal Times* was shot at as she was entering her office in Itanagar. The AHRC in its report further revealed:

From 1993 till date, seven journalists have been shot dead in Manipur.

Vicious attacks and bombings have become a part of their working environment. Media personnel live with harassment and threat on a daily basis. This has resulted in suspension of publication, blank editorials, and demands to the government for a safe working environment. In the case of five of the seven deceased journalists, no action and no arrests had resulted. From September 1997 to August, 2013, 29 FIRs in connection with harassment of journalists by underground groups have been filed in Manipur out of which 24 remain unresolved. In terms of harassment of journalists in Manipur by State/Central forces, 18 cases have been registered and 11 of these cases remain unresolved.

In Manipur, the entire print media had to stop publication of newspapers on three different occasions in 2007 because of the diktats of militant groups. Newspapers of Manipur have also felt obliged to carry blank editorial columns in the face of 'impossible' diktats from the government.

There are also instances of state government cutting down the government advertisements to the local media which are overtly critical of the government and try to highlight corruption in high places.

Then there are some powerful civil organisations who often behave like a law unto themselves and generally media never dare to indulge even in constructive criticism of them. Occasionally, whenever they do, it is invariably countered with brute aggression.

Being on the razor's edge, media loses its independence and become susceptible to compromise. This predicament was summed up by a very respected and veteran journalist of the region, Dhirendra Nath Bezbaruah, in the following words:

One cannot expect the journalists to be martyrs every time. Understandably, compromises will continue to be made and journalistic ethics will continue to decline when no one is willing to ensure the security of brave journalists who refuse to compromise[6].

References

1   Vashum R. Nagas' Rights to Self Determination: An Anthropological-Historical Perspective, Mittal Publications.

2   Business Line, August 2, 2011

3   Shillong Times, October 1, 2013

4   Deccan Herald, February 18, 2014)

5   The Hindu April 26, 2014

6   Dialogue, July-September, 2010, Vol. 12 (1)

Reporting Northeast India

TERESA REHMAN

As I came out of the Chief Judicial Magistrate's office after deposing before the Judicial Magistrate in Guwahati on the infamous story on a 'fake encounter' in Manipur, which I did for a news magazine some years back, I saw a outside broadcasting (OB) van of a television crew standing outside. A group of enthusiastic young reporters were waiting to cover a rally outside the Court.

As the voice of the agitators became shriller, the excitement level grew among the journalists. I could figure out that the reporters were mostly fresh graduates, barely out of their teens, excited to go live on air. Many of them would not be aware of the harsh realities a journalist reporting hardcore conflict faces. For instance, wearing a protective gear, knowing the legal aftermath of a story and basic things like how to be on the safe side, both mentally and physically. These are the harsh realities in the life of a journalist in a conflict zone and unfortunately no media school prepares them for this.

The impact of such continuous and live coverage of war and conflict is summed up in this quote from Mark Miller, author of 'How TV Covers War', in the book, *New Challenges for Documentary*, edited by Alan Rosenthal (University of California, 1998):

> "Watching the news, we come to feel not only that the world is blowing up, but that it does so for no reason, that its ongoing history is nothing more than a series of eruptions, each without cause or context. The news creates this vision of mere anarchy through its erasure of the past and its simultaneous tendency to atomise the present into so many unrelated happenings, each recounted through a series of dramatic, unintelligible pictures".

Apart from the 'news' dished out to us by the 24X7 news channels, there are many aspects of journalism which seem to fade away from public discourse and even the curriculum of the media schools which have grown all over India. More importantly, nobody talks about the trauma that a journalist faces. The safety of a journalist, especially in a country like India, is never a priority. I still remember when I was attending the first regional conference of South Asia Women In Media (SAWM) in Lahore, Pakistan, senior Pakistani journalist Munizae Jehangir asked me, "Do you wear bullet-proof jackets when you go reporting?" This question jolted me the realities which I had confronted during my reporting assignments.

Tongam Rina, Associate Editor of *The Arunachal Times* was shot at while she was about to enter her office at Itanagar, the capital of Arunachal Pradesh in July 2012. She had told me that there is not enough for attending to the trauma of journalists reporting from conflict zones in India as well as South Asia. She said, "There is none, apart from few individuals coming to your help. You are pretty much left on your own devices. I was in a better position than lot of others since I had colleagues from all over the country that truly cared about me. You are left traumatized for a long period of time and you don't know who to approach. Either you completely withdraw or you are upset and become a nervous wreck, compounded by the fact that there is not much support at hand. Physical pain goes away but it is the mental pain that stays with you. And sadly, I don't know of an organization that attends to the trauma of the journalists. I wish that things change and someone get trained and take up the cause."

I still remember the distraught mother of a 'child soldier' recruited by a militant outfit who was wailing incessantly. Sitting in the courtyard of her home in Thoubal district of Manipur, an insurgency-ravaged state in Northeast India, she narrated how her 12-year-old son went out to play after school and never came back. There were several children like her son who were lured on some pretext or the other and recruited by a militant outfit. The outfit later declared that these children had joined them out of their own consent!

She took me inside her sparsely decorated living room and took out his school bag and showed his books, his sketches and his colour pencils which he was so fond of. As a woman journalist reporting from a conflict-zone, I had to curb my emotions and ask the distressed woman the usual grueling questions. And I had a feeling she could see my empathy and opened up. It took her some time though.

And then came my brush with terror. The Manipur Police Commandos, well known for their human rights abuses, surrounded the house. I could see eyes peeping through the open windows. One of their commanders came in. He started questioning the lady about me and checked my identity card, apologised and left. The commander told the lady in his native language that he thought I was a 'mediator.' For a moment I held my breath and heaved a sigh of relief when they left.

The person accompanying me told me that I was fortunate that they at least stopped to ask. The state is under the draconian Armed Forces (Special Powers) Act of 1958 which gives security forces unrestricted and unaccounted power to carry out their operations once an area is declared disturbed. Even a non-commissioned officer is granted the right to shoot to kill based on mere suspicion that it is necessary to do so in order to "maintain the public order.

An advantage of being a journalist reporting from a conflict zone is that one gets to see both sides of the coin. And as a journalist, one has to be objective and see the other side of the story, which often is eclipsed by drab government press releases on the number of militants killed and the number of arms and ammunition recovered. I almost feel that journalists can actually act as a bridge and go to the root of the complex issues that leads a young kid barely out of his or her teens to take up an AK-47 without batting an eyelid.

It's an irrefutable fact that journalists working in this violence-scarred region, especially in Manipur and Nagaland, are constantly flirting with danger. In a state like Manipur, where over 20 different underground outfits operate, editors have been killed by unidentified gunmen and journalists stopped from doing their jobs by militant outfits that have gone to the extent of closing down newspaper offices. Media persons often have to face the wrath of both the underground outfits and government agencies, including the security forces.

The need for the media to have a sense of history, of perspective, and of independence becomes imperative in situations where the victims are also the powerless, those who have no access to the media and, through it, to the decision-makers.

Times have also begun to change for the militants of the Northeast. It's now easy to visualise a gun-toting militant sitting with a laptop in the middle of his camp in the forests of Manipur, Nagaland or Assam, e-mailing press releases to the media. As we ill-equipped journalists grapple with the hostile terrain and psychological barriers that accompany dealing with complex insurgency operations, cyber-savvy militants shoot out press releases, e-newsletters and even threats to mediapersons and prominent personalities via e-mail! ULFA's publicity secretary, who writes under the pseudonym 'Rubi Bhuyan', even engaged in a debate on one of Assam's e-groups.

Many big-time militant groups have impressive websites and boast computer engineers among their cadres. Today's cyber age allows them to communicate with the media, which acts as a force multiplier for underground outfits for whom coverage is otherwise hard to come by. Militants are easily able to access Internet editions of newspapers and read what's been written about them; news establishments also provide them tip-offs about impending army operations. The Internet has, in fact, become the militants' latest tool to communicate with the outside world and seek solidarity for their cause.

There is now a definite and marked change in the manner in which the media and cyber-savvy militants operate. The Northeast is home to a number of militant groups, some prosperous, many rag-tag. Of late, it has become fashionable for media persons to be invited to militant camps so that they can dish out 'exclusive' news to those watching thousands of miles away. I myself have travelled to several militant camps for a first-hand experience of the gun-toting, lower-rung cadres as well as their top leaders.

Militant outfits are equally media-savvy, and now-a-days it is not unusual to receive emailed press releases from them. As I began to write this piece, I had been reading an e-mailed press release sent by a militant outfit in the region. I recall what Sunil Nath, a surrendered militant, had told me once. Nath was the publicity secretary of the United Liberation Front of Asom (ULFA). He told me how the militant outfits were conscious of the power of the media and the publicity wing was one of their most important wings. He recalled how in 1989, the banned outfit had first acquired its prized possession – an Apple Macintosh for a steep price of 1.5 lakh rupees from Dhaka, the capital of Bangladesh. It was kept a secret and few in the outfit knew of its existence. Prior to that, the militant groups used human couriers to deliver messages, which was not safe for them. But the Internet changed things and they could break across geographical barriers to send across their message to the outside world, especially the media.

It is intriguing to report from a conflict zone, but it has its share of perils. It's a tightrope for us 'combat' journalists as we have to grapple with threats from both the state and non-state actors. I had exposed a fake encounter by the state police in broad daylight in Manipur's capital Imphal. A local photographer who was present at the site took minute-by-minute pictures of the gory incident and was petrified of publishing it in the local papers. Not caring for the scoop of a lifetime, he sent it to us and the story sparked off angry protests and a civil uprising in the state.

The story won global acclaim, but for me, doing the story was a traumatic experience. I was not just an objective journalist here but also a woman and a mother. The photographs haunted me. I had sleepless nights. It's not just the physical dangers that we have to combat but also the psychological trauma, which often goes unnoticed. And to top it off, there are no support services for counselling a traumatised journalist. A journalist friend tells me that it's a myth that journalists have to be tough. Reporting from a conflict zone has a fear factor which is 'real'. I would be lying if I said that I did not get scared while reporting from a conflict zone. It's an undeniable fact that journalists working in this troubled region, especially in Manipur and Nagaland, are constantly flirting with danger. Mediapersons often have to face the wrath of both the underground outfits and government agencies, including the security forces.

The Northeast has often been misrepresented by the so-called 'mainstream' national media. Mediapersons reporting in this region have an important responsibility to alter the stereotypical manner in which the Northeast is represented in the media. With globalisation, the region has witnessed a surge in media activity, with a growing number of vernacular and local dailies, including four private television channels. There has also been a boom in FM radio stations, most of them entertainment-driven.

There are several faces of this militancy-ravaged region which have to be brought into the public domain. The Northeast is clubbed together as a homogeneous whole, a trouble-torn frontier that must be protected at all costs. It is therefore a challenge for media persons reporting from the field to act as a catalyst in creating an understanding between the State and non-State actors. We need to find a solution for the long-drawn-out conflict and analyse what it is that makes young boys and girls, barely out of their teens, take up arms without batting an eyelid.

Terror in these parts, especially in Manipur and Nagaland, is all-pervasive. But in spite of the perils, persons from the media have to be sensitive and perceptive to the real issues. It is important that someone sitting in Delhi or Mumbai knows that there is a lady called Irom Sharmila in Manipur who has been fasting for the past eight years demanding a repeal of the Armed Forces (Special Powers) Act of 1958.

I remember an interesting conversation with Ima Gyaneswari, one of the 12 elderly mothers of Manipur who were catapulted to fame when they stripped and held a banner across their bare bodies, challenging the army to rape them if they had the guts, right in front of the headquarters of the Assam Rifles. Gyaneswari, a wife and mother, smiled as she narrated the events of that fateful day.

She told me she is so traditional, she touches her husband's feet whenever she goes out for an important function. On that particular day however, she simply told him she was taking part in a protest. When she thinks about it now she feels it was a 'do-or-die' situation for her and her associates; she had to protect the daughters of Manipur. Her husband and her sons later reconciled to the fact that what she did was indeed courageous. Gyaneswari believes that the army has become more sensitised in their dealings with women. But she wants the draconian Armed Forces (Special Powers) Act of 1958 to go.

Gyaneswari admits that although the daring act received widespread media coverage, it did not have the desired effect on the authorities. She was amused and touched by my questions. She said nobody had ever tried to delve into their psyche and understand why these mothers of Manipur had done what they did. This was the first time someone had asked her to speak her heart out.

It is becoming increasingly pertinent to analyse conflict reportage, especially with the growth of the reach and the power of the media in India. This is especially true in conflict-torn areas like the Northeast of India, Jammu and Kashmir, Chattisgarh etc. The media curriculum, especially in these region should be tailored to meet the needs of the situation. The young budding journalists should be trained on the various aspects of conflict reportage – including the physical and psychological trauma that a journalist is exposed to. It is also important to train journalists to be sensitive to the local situations, have a basic knowledge of the history of the conflict and the society of the area covered.

Media and Insurgency

SAMUDRA GUPTA KASHYAP

"I envy you, boss! There are so many insurgent groups in the Northeast that there is no end to stories from there!" – This was how a Delhi-based journalist greeted me when a common friend and fellow journalist introduced me to him in the Press Club in the national capital a few years ago. The poor chap thought all we – reporters and other journalists in the Northeastern region – do is wait for an abduction, an explosion, a police briefing or a press note from the militant groups – nowadays an e-mail, and our daily job is done!

Well, having been in the business of reporting about the Northeastern region for the past 34 years—twenty-three of which has been for a national newspaper like *The Indian Express* – I am sometimes tempted to think that my New Delhi-based friend was correct. I know many journalists, both *local* and *outsider* – emphasis definitely deliberate – who still believe that insurgency, violence, terror, abduction and killings are the only *news* happening in the Northeast India. It was only a couple of years ago that the editor of a now defunct Guwahati-based newspaper had taken the trouble of travelling – mostly on foot through jungles– for several days to meet ULFA armed wing chief Paresh Barua in his hideout in Myanmar to come out with a wonderful series on the fugitive rebel. I am not trying to dismiss my friend's story – the first ever interview of that particular rebel leader that was serialized in the newspaper. But the fact remains that the common man in Assam, who was once almost totally enamoured by Paresh Barua & Co, are now least bothered about them. Had this interview been taken say 10 years ago, things would have been different.

As a reporter I consider myself lucky to have had the rare opportunity of seeing the rise of a militant group like United Liberation Front of Asom

(ULFA) as also its gradual fade-out. Looking back to the insurgency movements in the Northeast, we find that while two major insurgency movements – Naga and Mizo insurgencies – had started much before, those remained mostly out of reach of the media which was then restricted only to the print medium. Moreover, absence of local media in the Naga Hills and Lushai Hills, and lack of concern among the so-called mainstream media of the country, had together restricted media reporting of those two major uprisings to government press releases and information occasionally given out by the police and security forces. Likewise, though insurgency had also emerged in Manipur as early as in 1964 (Naga insurgency however had already made footing in the hills there), there was hardly any media coverage except for 'incidents' where militants were involved.

I am not trying to draw a historical or chronological note on insurgency-reporting in the Northeast. The background however remains that while initially the Kolkata press had some space for the insurgent movements of the region, it was only in the late 1970s that the media – print media – had actually 'arrived' to cover the troubles in the Northeast. Those however again were mostly government-fed information, with little being written about the why and how of the movements. About space for the plight of the common, the historical reason behind these movements, large-scale violation of human rights by security forces as well as by the rebel groups – the less said the better. It was not until Oinam ('Operation Bluebird') happened in 1987 in Manipur that human rights violation actually became news.

The development of mass media has had a tremendous impact on our lives especially in the past five decades. Even in a country like India where literacy had crossed the 50 per cent mark only three decades ago, two important development-related campaigns – green revolution and malaria-eradication – became possible solely because of the mass media. The present generation will sue find it difficult to understand how the illiterate Indian farmer made the best use of urea and super-phosphates in their fields by listening to the transistor radio set that had once become inseparable from Indian rural life.

I don't want to get into what Maoist theory says of insurgency and mass support. But it is a fact that insurgent groups have come to use the media as an effective tool to carry forward their cause, so much so that most groups across the globe have even coerced – if not co-opted – the media to carry their message as the gospel truth. We have numerous instances of journalists being killed by insurgent groups across the globe, and the Northeastern region is no exception. Daniel Pearl, Steven Sotloff, Kamala Saikia, R K Sanatomba, Lalrohlu Hmar, Thounaojam Brajamani Singh, Konsam Rishikanta…, the list is long.

There were also allegations – which fortunately remained unsubstantiated in most cases – of media-persons taking the side of insurgent groups in Assam and Manipur, with this allegation coming mostly from the government. Several editors and other journalists have been also arrested, detained under draconian laws like TADA, as also harassed for their alleged but unproved 'connections' with insurgent groups.

Reporting insurgency has always remained a difficult task both within the region and outside. Within the region journalists are always under various kinds of pressures, from both sides – the government and security forces as well as the insurgent groups. We are all familiar with the kind of challenges the media fraternity has been facing in Manipur. On one side the government does not want the media to give space to the rebels, on the other side the militant groups want their statements published ad verbatim. The situation has become worse when some factions started exerting pressure on the media not to publish statements issued by their rival groups.

I recently had a quick look at some reviews of an interesting book titled, *Media War: The Media-Enabled Insurgency in Iraq* (ProSIM Company, Inc.; 1st edition (December 18, 2010) written by Lieutenant Colonel Pat Proctor (US Army) is a veteran of both the Iraq and Afghanistan wars.

As Proctor pointed out, the Iraq War did not happen so much in Baghdad or al-Anbar as the world believes. Instead, it happened every day on television, in newspapers, and on the Internet. "It was the struggle between the US military and the insurgency for the will of the American people to prosecute the war. And the US military lost."

"How could the US military, the most powerful military force in the history of the world, be forced out of Iraq by 'bands of thugs and terrorists'? It was not, as others have contended, bad strategic decisions, poor military planning or execution, or a biased or negligent media that made the enemy in Iraq so formidable. Rather, it was the revolutionary merging of terrorism, insurgency, and telecommunications: media-enabled insurgency."

Proctor then asks a very pertinent question: Does media-enabled insurgency exist? The book brings about some examples of the 'enemy' using the media to illustrate that media-enabled insurgency does exist and the 'enemy' was using it. And then he goes on to ask: what is the mechanism by which the 'enemy's' tactical attacks are translated into changes in public opinion through the media? He also refers to specific incidents to show that the 'enemy' operates at the event and collection level of the media system, producing pictures and data, generating events and controlling access to influence news stories about the operational area. Finally, is media-enabled insurgency a threat? It seems, media-enabled insurgency threatens to prevent the US military from achieving its objectives in Iraq.

Picking up ideas from Proctor, I would also say, groups are not entirely and exclusively media-enabled insurgency. Rather they use media-enabled insurgency for various reasons. One, it is one way to survive and prove that they are alive and kicking. Two, they must build image and attract recruits. Three, they have to push other groups out, increase their clout and thus extort more money. Four, it must terrorise or ingratiate itself to the local population in order to remain hidden and take shelter whenever required. And finally, to exert pressure on the government.

Permit me to go step by step on the Northeast experience of insurgency and media. Let us be very frank; Half a century of Counter-Insurgency Operations in the region, but the government has failed to evolve a clear media policy. The Media still seen as nuisance, if not an aberration. I am not saying that the media should be used for CI-CT operations; but had there been a clear official media policy vis-à-vis insurgency, these groups would not got such long tenures of existence, and hundreds of innocent lives would have been sad. Just one example: the entire Assam media came down heavily on the ULFA following the explosion in Dhemaji on Independence Day, 2004 where 12 little children were killed. But the government failed to strike when the iron was hot.

Broadly looking, the government has always resorted to knee-jerk reactions to incidents triggered off by the insurgents, and then comfortably accuses the media of providing much-needed oxygen to the groups. Yes, media is oxygen to the insurgent groups; they cannot survive without the media. Media is a powerful component in conflict situations across the globe, and the Northeastern region is no exception. A unique dynamic emerges in media operation in conflict situations, primarily due to two reasons: First, conflict situations globally have extraordinary news value; thus attracts media focus. Second, security implications of conflict imbue such reportage with utmost public importance and interest.

The fact is, everybody needs the media. Terrorist and insurgent groups consistently attempt to draw attention of media. By doing so, insurgent groups also attract attention of decision-makers and the common people. Similarly, governments also utilize media to build public opinion against violence and terrorism. Thus, the media is a significant construct both to the terrorists and the state. But this is not exactly happening in the Northeast.

Operation Bajrang (Nov 1990) in Assam is a classic illustration. It failed to inform media on time and with accuracy. This resulted in local resentment and ill-informed reporting in the media. The Army and its operations were seen in poor light. The ULFA used human right groups to cry hoarse against Army. With no idea about the local media, the security forces, whose primary responsibility was to work for protection of the common man, got very poor media projection. Public perception and public opinion went against the security forces. About one year later, Operation Rhino (September 1991) improved on lessons learnt. A tendency to include Media as part of operations gradually developed. But again, there was a tendency to get national media coverage instead of reaching out to the local communities who were worst victims of insurgency. Moreover, most media engagements continued to be personality-driven.

But gradually the scenario changed. The army started reaching out to local media. One-to-one interactions began. Officers were gradually permitted to talk to media, though in a limited manner. A PRO was appointed in Guwahati for two-way flow of information. Tactical HQ officer was also began to interact with media. And, in about two years, media access to the Army's Corps HQ was finally opened.

But thanks to learning from past mistakes, there has been a new dynamics of change. One indicator of new dynamics of change in media-military relationship in an insurgency situation is the gradual discarding of the term "Media Management." There is realization that media cannot be 'managed' ('paid news' is still not an epidemic!). Media cannot be hoodwinked or fooled. Media after all is a pillar of democracy as also vital oxygen to it.

The Insurgent groups too know that media is Oxygen to terrorists. They too need the media, and in fact need it much more than security forces do. Terrorists need publicity, usually free publicity that a group cannot normally afford or buy. Terrorists want publicity for the following reasons:

(i)   To gain attention,

(ii)   To inspire fear and respect,

(iii)   To secure favourable understanding of their cause, if not their act,

(iv)   To create a favourable understanding of their cause, if not their act,

(v)   They may also seek to court, or place, sympathetic personnel in press positions,

(vi)   They want the media to give legitimacy to what is often portrayed as ideological or personality feuds or divisions between armed groups and political wings,

(vii)   They want the media to notice and give legitimacy to findings and viewpoints of specially-created NGOs and study centers,

(viii) In hostage situations, they need details on identity, number and value of hostages, as also details of pending rescue attempts,

(ix)   They want media coverage that causes damage to their enemy,

(x)   They want the media to amplify panic, to spread fear,

(xi)   They want to facilitate economic loss (like scaring away investment and tourism),

(xii) They want to make people lose faith in the government's ability to protect them, and finally,

(xiii) They want to trigger off government and popular over-reaction to specific incidents and overall threat of terrorism.

What the government could have done in such situations? Seek understanding, cooperation, restraint, and loyalty from media. This is intended to limit terrorist harm to society and make efforts to punish or apprehend those responsible for terrorist acts. Governments want media coverage to advance government agenda and not that of the terrorist, but there is no clear-cut policy. The government could have tried to separate terrorists from the media and deny them a publicity platform. There is always ample scope to present terrorists as criminals and win over the media to stop glamorizing them. There are scopes to foster the viewpoint that kidnapping a prominent person, blowing up a building, or hijacking an airplane is a criminal act regardless of the terrorists' cause. There could have been strategies to control terrorist access to outside data. Governments do desire that media don't reveal current anti-terrorist actions & plans that provide the terrorists with data that helps them, but there is no policy to translate this desire into reality.

These are only some ideas that have come to my mind, having had the opportunity to interact with five major stakeholders caught in the insurgency situation, these being the government, security forces, insurgent groups, intelligentsia and of course the media. More ideas can emanate through further discussions.

Media's Role in Facilitating Peace in Conflict Situations in Assam

RAJEEV BHATTACHARYYA

Before assessing the scenario in Assam, it is imperative to analyse whether the media actually has or should have a role in facilitating peace in conflict situations. Over the past few decades, diverse opinions have been articulated from different quarters on the issue. The origin of this debate can be traced to the mid 1960s when some Norwegian dailies were evaluated for their coverage of the crises in Congo, Cuba and Cyprus. In the subsequent decades, the media's role came in for further scrutiny during the genocide in Rwanda, the conflict in Yugoslavia, the upheavals in Fiji, Vanuatu and Papua New Guinea and the pro-independence insurrection in New Caledonia. The discussions seemed to make a case that journalists ought to be facilitators of peace in conflict situations.

Not surprisingly, this approach has generated debate and controversy—should the media always stay detached, even from dreadful events unfolding around them, or should it adopt a position as suggested by a section of scholars and become attached to a cause such as promoting peace? Journalists belonging to the traditional school of thought are of the firm opinion that subscribing to "peace journalism" could put an end to objectivity in news reporting and that journalists would take sides in a conflict. And the dangers of taking sides are quite obvious—professional independence would be impossible to maintain, access to the other sides' combatants would disappear and journalists would become even more of a target than they already are.

However, advocates of "peace journalism" argue that their ideas are suitable and not difficult to follow when the purpose of reportage is to generate social harmony and freedom. In the same vein, they affirm that the coverage of conflicts should be "people-oriented" in the sense that focus should be on the victims and giving a voice to the voiceless. It is also truth-oriented in that the untruth on all sides is revealed by getting access to events and themes that usually remain concealed from public view. Peace journalism cautions the media from being manipulated by opinion makers and even makes a case for coverage of "blood and guts stories" that could be appalling to some viewers.

From 1978, as many as four consultative meetings were held by working journalists from all over the world under the auspices of UNESCO on "professional ethics." In 1983, a declaration was issued that a true journalist should stand for objective reality, democracy, peace, human rights etc, among other goals. In fact, no professional journalist would ever deny that the very practice of good professional journalism is in itself a form of conflict resolution – or at least is something that has parallels to conflict resolution. It is quite possible that a consensus can be arrived at on certain parameters in any conflict situation. The provision of accurate information is a priority for all journalists as also maintaining a culture of professional journalism.

The debate notwithstanding, it must be accepted that the media's role in a given conflict or in any other situation depends on a complex set of factors. This may be determined by the relationship the media has to actors in the conflict and the independence the media has vis-à-vis power brokers in society. Very often, there is pressure to focus on the immediate and dramatic events which is especially true of broadcast journalism. This could often be at the expense of explaining the background and issues that may have sparked the conflict. Moreover, not all conflicts are given equal importance or covered extensively by the media. Undoubtedly, the political significance of some conflicts affects the reaction of the governments and this in turn may affect the media's coverage of such conflicts.

The situation in Assam had been no different where conflict escalated sharply from 1990 when counter-insurgency operations were launched by the army against the United Liberation Front of Asom (ULFA) which claimed to be fighting for the state's independence from India. The media in the state was acquainted with covering conflict since the state had been hit by violence at regular intervals in the previous decades. The historic Assam Movement (1979-85) against foreign nationals provoked violence between different communities. But what was witnessed in the subsequent two decades was conflict of a different kind when the authority of the state was challenged and there was organized violence between ethnic groups. The media also began to assume a more important and challenging role.

The media was caught off-guard by the quick turn of events from 27 November 1990 when the Asom Gana Parishad (AGP) government was dismissed for its inability to check the ULFA and President's Rule was imposed in the state. A day later, the army began a crackdown against the rebel outfit by launching Operation Bajrang. In the absence of actionable intelligence, the army could not firm up an effective strategy and the top rung leadership had already escaped even before their hideouts were raided in Saraipung and Lakhipathar. According to former ULFA functionaries, some army personnel were killed either as a result of encounters or by landmines as they zeroed in on these locations. Enraged with the setback, the army unleashed a reign of terror on the civilian populace residing in the nearby villages.

The media was not allowed access to the affected zones. Still, some journalists managed to dig out information on the atrocities which were covered in the local dailies. Around the same time, the army discovered a mass grave of decomposed bodies at the ULFA camp in Lakhipathar. The victims were people who had been arrested and given capital punishment by the rebel outfit for offences like poaching, human trafficking, spying, etc. Realising the importance of the media and dissemination of information, the army seized upon the opportunity and took a group of journalists to the spot. In much the same way as the violence perpetrated by the army was covered, the brutal conduct of ULFA was splashed for days on the front page of most dailies. ULFA had cultivated a sort of Robin Hood image for itself in Assam and it was increasingly viewed as the panacea to all the ills afflicting the state. News stories on the mass grave and about people being slaughtered brutally in the camps gave a severe jolt to the image of the insurgent group.

That the ULFA rested on weak fundamentals was apparent a few months after the army launched the offensive. Cadres from many districts bid adieu to militancy and returned to the mainstream. The organization was in disarray and it could never anticipate the fallout of operations on such a large scale. To take advantage of the situation, the government offered a rehabilitation package to the militants who came overground but its sinister act of staging fake surrenders was soon unraveled by the media. Editorials in some dailies were even of the opinion that the total number of rebels who surrendered in 1992 had been more than the total number of cadres in the ranks of ULFA! In fact the tradition of fake surrenders that was inaugurated by the government continued unabated for more than a decade. Media reports were published at regular intervals highlighting the phenomenon until the ministry of home affairs came out with strict guidelines on such 'surrenders' in 2008.

Within a few months of the Congress sweeping to power in 1991, another operation called Operation Rhino was launched against ULFA. But it was different in tone and tenor from the previous exercise in certain aspects which was only partially successful. The army realized that counter-insurgency operations were as much a war of information as it was about fighting with guns and bullets. Unlike the previous occasion, the army cooperated with the police and availed the services of former rebels. The results were naturally encouraging but in the midst of all these operations were human rights violations and fake encounters. One such incident which created sensation after being highlighted by the media happened in Nagaon in 1994 when five suspected ULFA cadres were gunned down and their bodies burned with tyres. A photographer's lens managed to capture a policeman pouring kerosene over the dead bodies before they were set on fire!

The offensive by the army notwithstanding, ULFA was able to regroup and establish bases in Bhutan, Bangladesh and Myanmar within a few years. Around the same time, another outfit Bodo Security Force (BSF) which was later renamed as the National Democratic Front of Bodoland unleashed a fierce campaign for independence of the Bodo inhabited areas in Assam. In addition to targeting security forces, it allegedly orchestrated attacks against non-Bodo communities such as the tea tribes. Many were killed and hundreds displaced from their homes. Before long, militancy also began to brew among the tea tribes with the emergence of the Birsa Commando Force and Adivasi Cobra Military of Assam.

Till the mid 1990s, the media had been by and large successful in portraying the ground reality of the different layers of the conflict in Assam. This is however not to suggest that all the dailies and weeklies were neutral and devoid of news stories that were exaggerated and unverifiable. Some could be even said to have taken sides in the conflict. A new weekly newspaper, for instance, had adopted a completely pro-ULFA stance which at times even justified some demands and activities of the banned group. A few senior journalists were also arrested and jailed for allegedly being pro-ULFA. These incidents apart, there was hardly any doubt that the media appeared more confident than ever before and it would not simply accept the versions doled out by the government or the rebel outfits. Many a time stories have punched holes in claims and counter-claims made by these agencies and groups.

There was a perceptible change in the coverage of conflicts in Assam from the late 1990s with the proliferation of daily newspapers and weeklies. According to information provided by the Department of Information and Public Relations (DIPR), there were as many as 26 dailies and 80 weekly magazines registered with the Government of Assam in 1999 although only a fraction of these publications was actually distributed and read. Nonetheless, the figure was much higher than in 1991 when there were only about ten dailies and ten weekly magazines. In a bid to increase circulation, some dailies began to feed on sensationalism which sometimes stretched to ridiculous limits. It is difficult to quantify the percentage of such stories that were published and a different picture would emerge if different dailies are taken into consideration. There have been instances when stories on a few incidents were carried on page one of some dailies for days together. This trend was discernible more in the vernacular than in the English dailies. Both catered to a different readership and the English reading community was more urban based and belonged to the middle class. For them, stability and cessation of violence was of greater interest than their continuation.

Incidentally, the late 1990s also coincided with an aggressive counter-offensive by the government against insurgent groups. Realising the role of the media in such operations, more journalists began to be co-opted by the army and other government agencies for a campaign in the media against the armed groups. Incidentally, journalists from the English and national media as well also figured in this group. The media was being used for a variety of purposes including psychological operations and misinformation at times. Not surprisngly, there was a greater dose of news attributed to "highly placed sources" or "reliable sources in the government" during this period which have continued till date. At times, spreading false news can wreak havoc among rebel outfits since communication is not always regular between commanders and cadres on the ground. And sometimes, media houses are fed information on issues that have made the rebel organizations unpopular among the masses. For instance, the link between ULFA and Pakistan's ISI was harped upon at regular intervals which manifested in a series of news articles in all the dailies. Some were true and some were false but journalists wrote whatever was given to them. Sometimes a small percentage of these inputs were proved correct by events as it happened during the Kargil War when ULFA's close links with Pakistan were established beyond doubt. But the possibility of verifying information received from security agencies and the rebel outfits had been always bleak. And the hazard of not filing the news in the evening would certainly be avoided by journalists since other dailies would publish them.

Even as the dailies competed among themselves to increase circulation, the emergence of TV news channels became a crucial factor in the coverage of conflict in Assam. While there had been only one TV channel in 2002, as many as six had sprung up by 2013. The scope of coverage of conflicts or any other event had always been less in the broadcast than the print media. TV focuses on current happenings unlike print which can also delve into the past of current events on a separate page. But there is hardly any doubt that there is a much greater impact from a story that is broadcast. And the reason is simple: seeing is believing. Once footage is telecast about an incident or situation, the viewers do not need to be convinced about the authenticity of the news story. And it is only natural that stories on TV have usually been published by dailies and magazines, sometimes with a bit of value addition and sometimes the exact version shown on screen. But this trend has had its share of negative and positive aspects.

Like the print media, there have been numerous occasions when the channels have telecast speculative and unverifiable stories. Such stories have been and are still being done without visual footage of the incident but by showing maps, bytes and old photographs. For instance, channels have been regularly broadcasting stories about rebel camps in Myanmar being shelled and destroyed by the army. And of course the source of the information would invariably be attributed to "intelligence sources" or "reliable government sources." Likewise, the channels have aired stories about Maoists being trained by the ULFA in Myanmar. Not only was this untrue but it transpired later on that ULFA had been working to ensure that the CPI (Maoist) did not spread in Assam. And once such stories are aired, most vernacular dailies invariably carry them the following day.

Perhaps the best example of speculative stories comes from the case of this author when a series of stories was broadcast and published when he had gone on a secret assignment to cover Myanmar's rebel bases in northern Sagaing Division. On 3 December 2011, a news channel said that the author and a senior ULFA functionary Jibon Moran had been apprehended by the Myanmarese army. Two days later, another channel said that the author would be released by the army at Tamu but his camera and recorder had been seized. A week later, some dailies said that the author had been detained by NSCN(K) president S S Khaplang at his camp and that a whopping Rs 5 crores was being demanded by the Naga rebel leader for his release. Nothing could have been more untrue; the author and his journalist colleague Pradip Gogoi were safe in the ULFA camp awaiting the arrival of its chief of staff Paresh Baruah. It transpired later on that the input was given by an intelligence agency to a news channel to ascertain if two journalists had actually gone to Myanmar to interview top rebel functionaries. Once these stories came on the channel, other media houses could not afford to avoid the story whether it was true of false.

Like the print media which is concerned over raising circulation, the race for increasing television rating point (TRP) has been the obsession with news channels. The more the TRP, the greater are the chances of advertisements and generation of revenue which is of greater importance for the broadcast media since expenditure is higher. Stories that should not have been focused upon on ethical grounds have been found to be shown repeatedly to gain more viewership. Footage that could easily exacerbate violence in a conflict situation were shown and discussions held by roping in experts in special programmes. This happened quite prominently in August 2014 when clashes erupted along the disputed Assam-Nagaland border in Golaghat. Many persons were killed as a result of attacks by miscreants and in firing by the police. Self-censorship which is considered an important ingredient in professional journalism is yet to be understood and practiced by the media in Assam. Most of the media houses are owned by politicians and businessmen and for whom fulfillment of their own agendas take precedence over everything else.

In spite of these limitations, TV journalism has brought into focus hitherto uncovered regions and aspects of conflicts in Assam. The channels have been tremendously aided by the cellular phone and advanced technologies (like WhatsApp now) that facilitate faster transfer of video and audio files. Very often footage has been found to be sent by ordinary citizens from remote areas where correspondents are not stationed. And once an exclusive story is aired by a channel, others are bound to follow suit and walk the extra mile for more information. The impact has been a greater understanding of the conflict in terms of its cause, impact and the roles of the different actors involved.

Entire world is not 'Outer Darkness': Need to Break Free

NIRENDRA DEV

South Asian history has no one beginning, no one chronology, no single plot or narrative. It is not a singular history, but rather many histories. Therefore, South Asia does not have a cultural and historical heartland. On the economic front, it is increasingly dead even though there's no dearth of natural potentials and availability of workforce.

But having said so, we must not miss the point that there's a social heartland. It's beyond cultural paradigm or political identity. The behaviours of Mizos, Nagas, Arunachal tribals and even in countries like Bangkok could be similar. I often say, look at the way, people in this region treat their guests.

'*Athithi Deva Bhava*' could be a Sanskrit or Aryan concept, but here in this region we implement it day in and day out. Born in Nagaland and educated in Nagaland, Mizoram and in Shillong; later in my professional career I have interacted with people from all over India, served in Nagaland, Delhi, Ahmedabad and Mumbai and have friends in Singapore and Thailand; no where I can bet friends and tourists, precisely the visitors to your home is treated as Gods as in our region.

But it's ironical that this quality of ours has not able to cement cordial relations between various groups, may be for whatever reasons and thus most conflicts are typically ethno-centric, tribal-non tribal or linguistic battles. We tend to suspect our immediate next door neighbours most.

The Naga tradition of head hunting is perhaps essentially due to that.

Virgin Land

That way, our region is a permanently virgin land for media. When goats die, it's the vultures that make the feast! But essentially, a newsman, I would not like to give up that right and liberty of a vulture.

As a newsperson I must go for the killing. And same would be my advise to the students of mass communication; never compromise on the lust to be 'vultures of news'. But we must use that right with immense sense of responsibility.

So, before, we get encircled ourselves with the issues about positive reporting and negative reporting; let me make it clear, I for one believe firmly that for a journalist or a newsperson, news is a news ! Either positive or negative should not bother us. It's not our cup of tea.

In other words, dog biting a man does not bother me even if the man is Narendra Modi or Rahul Gandhi; but the man biting the dog would make me jump from my bed. And ladies; if a woman bite a dog – it is bound to be bigger news.

I have mentioned above that with this liberty comes a bigger responsibility. We can also look at how readers have graduated themselves to be Consumers of News and Views.

Essentially, we ought to fall back on the basic teachings of journalism. With most students, this is known as a mere theory today but these have all time relevance. I am talking about the basics A, B, C. Accuracy, Balance and Clarity of news reporting.

If we can protect these three essential facets, our work as newspersons is done – more than half - smoothly and safely. Importantly, this is easier said than done.

Sometime the facts could be hazy, so Accuracy could be a difficult proposition. You would not get the other version to the story making Balance a casualty and thus Clarity would be far from achieved.

In conflict situations, these become more frequent. Someone who takes pride in saying that I started journalism from Kohima in Nagaland, I can also tell you things were no different when I covered Gujarat 2002 mayhem. So, our response to the situations has to be unique in each different situation; sometime unique each different way on daily basis. When I interact with young journalism and mass communication students in Delhi, I therefore give importance to tell them two things --- Meticulous reading and cultivating good respectable and dependable sources.

Uncle Google is neither; but we need him all the time.

Placing ourselves In the Heart of Things:

In 2002, my uncle Google was not as active as he is today. So as a non-Gujarati, I could function in the then Narendra Modi's Gujarat and his 6 crore Gujarati people, solely because friends came in to my help. The fellow journalists, police officers and so on. As a hunting bird, first two days I spent to locate someone with eastern India background; there was an Assamese IPS officer and he turned out to be MY MAN. This is just to give an example. There were others also.

In conflict situations, say riots and insurgency killings etc, we journalists should place us in the heart of the happenings. Meaning, no body should be killed without your knowledge….literally.

Getting hold of that information helps. You ought to know, who are the main actors, who killed whom, who retaliated where and how.

In conflict situation as in northeast or far East Asia, journalists have another crucial task to handle. I say, there is a fundamental lesson; media persons should follow here, do not lie to yourselves.

When I say, we should not 'lie' to own-self; please try to appreciate my focus. We in the media too have often failed in our duties towards the northeast India.

There's no gainsay in pointing out that northeast India has remained neglected zone from the power that be – that is New Delhi – it is only recently that due to economic and political compulsions, the Government of India has started to pay some extra attention and also lately charted out a Look East Policy.

For decades, to a credulous northeasterner, the world comes packaged through television, glossy magazines etc. Today's social networking sites have added to the excitement to both sides.

But still, people in northeast India and also to an extent the people of Myanmar are often called 'rebels' or guerillas. Issues of corruption, drug menace and AIDS are now being added to that image.

This brings us to a stage where somebody has to do the turning and walking first. Instead of always feeling let down by the mainstream India, there is a necessity to reach out. This needs to be encouraged and emulated.

New Age Media

Now coming to the issue of 'new age media.' The media these days have also started appealing not only to readers, but there is another community called consumers of news and views.

So, pristine seclusion in the hills, unspoiled and pastoral innocence of our people can no longer be the only virtue. The new age media calls for a situation when people of northeast India needs to accommodate themselves to the people of India, the neighbouring countries and the rest of the world.

The fact that India has returned to single party majority under a supposed hard task master Narendra Modi or that Bangladesh will be soon 45-year-old or what's happening around BRICS should interest a northeastern man. The crisis in Ukraine and the Arab Spring of 2012 are all events whose ramifications reach the northeast India and neighbouring countries. Thus, to put it emphatically, my Mantra is we need to open up more.

The journalists in northeast India needs to open up first with their fellow colleagues across the northeast and also in key South Asian and East Asian countries. I would like to suggest creation of a 'newspool' first among media persons in the region and then we could co-opt people from other places like Delhi, Kolkata, Dacca, Kathmandu, Singapore, Mumbai, Bangkok etc.

The onus is also on the media persons to take some leads. It's a reality, the new world and the new internet media cannot be kept at bay. Instead, we must take advantage of the same. We know there is still lot of paranoia among our people. There is a traditional mindset of reactionary resistance to all things that is not native.

Let us come back to the issue of what and how media should help out the people of this conflict-ridden region. Many years back legendary Homen Borgohain, a senior writer, had told me a fascinating thing that while places like Patna has a British Council Library and Bhopal had an official French cultural centre. But we have none of these institutes in the northeast. I am born and brought up in Nagaland; but have I contributed enough least to set up a similarly gigantic Library in Dimapur or Kohima? We, journalists, must gaze in inside sometime.

Economic Limitation

Now let us examine the economic limitations notwithstanding the resources as referred above.

The theory often circulated that the Government of India would deliver the moon; that the region will be en route to accelerating growth once Look East Policy is implemented so far remains only a fable.

In terms of economy, northeast remains rooted in some kind of stagnation. But it is in the will of the people and their hard work with focused approach that this region too like some nations can bounce from horrible recessionary lows.

But such a miracle is not possible first in isolation and secondly without hard work of the natives. So let us take some important issues point by point.

Firstly, the media needs to project what are the contributing factors that can help a stagnant economy like in this northeastern India to bounce back.

The region will probably bounce back if it can exploit the natural resources, promote organic farming, horticulture and develop the cottage industry in most of its varieties to tap the export market. Are we in the media doing enough on this?

The news pool I have spoken above can do a lot on these. Developments can undoubtedly help bring in peace and vice versa and an intra-regional news pool I am suggesting can highlight positive aspects in one state for the information and benefits of other states in the region. It can create market for finished products within the region and also jobs.

But have we so far done enough? Has the media in the region able to force people to do deep soul searching? Has it raised the right questions to get try get the right answers to help solve certain 'solvable' issues?

For instance, we in the northeast love to give each other the reputation of hardworking and disciplined people. But are we also not easy going and pleasantly disorderly lot? There has been another social lacuna which the media seldom pointed out or pointed out in the manner they should have. Generally speaking the innocence also leads our people in this region not to admit what has gone wrong. Forget politicians, even social activists and influential students' bodies too most of the times have been obsessively insecure about admitting failures.

Media has a responsibility to address these. In this context, let us the cite the role of All Assam Students' Union agitation and how they let such a mass-level agitation turn into a Bengal-kheda stir. How the AGP leaders were bound to fail as they stormed into the corridors of power with inexperience and at the same time selfish-motives to occupy best of rooms in the Dispur secretariat?

Has the media done enough work also to realize and then point out that between the locals in our region and the mainstream India, the politicians and the Government of India in particular, even the development issues often became the source of *dissent and conflict.*

During my stay in Nagaland in early 1990s, I have often heard local politicians telling that Government of India has been making roads in Nagaland only to help smoother movement of the Indian army.

The Indian army wanted the bushes cleared and proper roads constructed to ensure smooth movements of the troops to strike at the insurgents' hideouts.

I am not denying that hideouts were hit by using the roads. But, more critically, could the media not point out that it's the roads that would bring in development and the use of roads for movement of armed forces would turn only symbolic if greater economic engagement starts along the roads and at the end of the roads?

In my book, '*The Talking Guns: North East India*', (Manas Publications, 2008) I have dealt at length on the issue of absence of work culture or rather more serious menace called White Collar Job Syndrome.

And here I quote an extract from the book: "once locals developed a fascination for government jobs, a new malady set in the society –I call it White Collar Job Syndrome (WCJS), where natives decided they should not do anything else other than managing a government job. And when government job reached a saturation point, there was hullabaloo about unemployment".

Nation Building

But having dwelt at length on the native shortcomings, I have a few issues from the other side of the table too. It's about the role of the so called 'outsiders'.

In more ways than one, the northeast India is becoming an urban society. The societies, primarily of the tribals, in the region are today bursting out of their agrarian roots. This has not happened in just the new century. As many as 20 years ago, in 1991, the glamour queen Pooja Bedi, who was invited to Kohima as chief guest for Miss Nagaland Beauty Contest, was moved to the extent that made her comment later that all her prejudiced concept about Nagas as a 'head hunting' community had vanished.

From a primordial economy, the region today is a telling picture and plethora of a different world. It's so much 'westernized' in many aspects that a visitor can easily discard the conventional tribal theory of the natives.

In last six decades, the region has evolved from a coherent but tribal values and custom-ridden social system to a fragmented and mobile society; and thus also materialistic.

A recent report from a NGO claimed that by the density criterion growing number of population in most of the states from Tripura, Nagaland, Mizoram, Meghalaya and Assam – either prefer to stay put in urban or semi-urban pockets.

In other words, the majority of northeast population is living in corners that require piped water supply, improved roads and the modern housing and entrepreneurship policies. According to social scientists, poverty and poorer economic conditions are often followed by stagnation. By that standard, the northeast society is far from stagnant despite the vexed problems of violent insurgencies and often incompetent administration practically by political class of all hues in all the states.

To many old timers; the region has in fact surpassed the aspirations of the founding fathers. "Our people are living a standard of life, our forefathers have never dreamt off," the illustrious Naga politician S C Jamir had said once adding like Nagaland, most other states in the region, were born out of tears and blood; "but when we look at the changes that have taken place around us, can we really say it was all in vain".

The philosophy would work for other states obviously. We ought to also debate on the role of the common citizens—including both the natives and the 'so called outsiders' from the rest of India.

Ironically, these outsiders have been given distinct names in all the states – Vais in Mizoram, Dhwakers in Meghalaya and Plain Manu in Nagaland.

What need to be stressed is that even the common Indians—Bihari labour force, Bengali and Malayalee white collar workers and Marwari business people – all are only seen by the natives as tools exploiting the Nagas and Mizos and the local resources.

This, native northeasterner and outsider (from mainland India) relationship, therefore deserves a closer look. The nation building cannot be left as an exclusive domain of the ill-advised political class and the ill-informed babus. So far, the common faceless Indians have contributed sparsely little to bring the natives of the northeast closer to the Indian nationhood.

The uprising seen in civil society movement lately is a pointer that common people can work together to bridge this gulf. The first move should come from the 'outsiders' as generally they are seen by the locals as true examples of the bunch of self-seeking people concentrating only in minting money – a test case of fishing out of troubled waters. Here again, media is a platform that can help improve people-to-people relationship.

Next, how do we address the issue of racial violence?

My take would be little different and some of you, if not most, could disagree with me.

Delhi's real problems are two-fold. The society is lacking 'social or community leadership'. Now the media in Delhi is so much engaged in reporting politics, *dharnas* and broad economic issues like FDI retail etc that there is hardly space and time to raise the right questions about social responsibility of the Denizens.

Reports suggest when Arunachal boy Nido was attacked in Lajpat Nagar area; none came forward to stop the angry young 'local Delhiites' take law in their own hands. Let us go a bit far and talk about the unfortunate rape of Nirbhaya in December 2012. My argument is perhaps the ill-fated girl would have survived the ordeal had she and her friend made use of Delhi Metro that night. Now, that's the issue of public transport.

Delhi has another problem: deeper concern is the state of virtual paralysis of law and order machineries and how there's 'no fear' in the minds of the wrong doers.

In fact, notwithstanding the Somnath Bharti-Delhi cops imbroglio during the short-lived Kejriwal government in 2013-14 in the national capital, many would say Delhi cops are hardly known for helping commoners or resolving cases affecting poor.

Police Reforms

If there's a need for a police reform in India, it's more so in Delhi. The issue is hanging fire since when Rajesh Pilot under P V Narasimha Rao in mid 1990s was Minister of State for Home.

I have raised the bogey of police reforms as these would be vital even in the northeast India. Even in this region 'majoritanism' problem of police force remains a matter of concern. Media in northeast has seldom addressed these issues and mostly focused only to attack the armed forces. It was actually playing back to the gallery. It goes without saying Political control and manipulation has resulted in subjecting state police in each state to the malaise of 'majoritanism'. Therefore, if the cops sided with Shiv Sainiks in Mumbai and remained dormant during 2002 anti-Muslim mayhem in Gujarat, there are many tales about 'double standards' of the cops in our northeastern region too.

Undoubtedly the media and the intellectuals have a role to point out at these maladies. It goes without saying that a society whose intellectuals and media – who ideally should function as a mirror – shy away from their responsibility is sure to go into a deep slumber if not a deeper chaos.

Moreover, northeast India is also a victim of a theory, which you cannot easily dismiss away. Material progress without proper intellectual grounding and ethical commitment can certainly spell imbalance. This has happened in the society. Some of the materialistic developments and comforts came very fast and as the old ethics of older generation died down slowly, the new generation, I am afraid, today is devoid of that essential ethical and moral cloak.

Therefore, corruption is today a hallmark and something taken for granted. In many tribal societies, corruption is an 'Indian vice'; but today it has turned into a reality. Thus, respect for moral authority and scholarship is eroding while an unlimited hypocrisy pervades as an order of the day.

Media, thus, has a role to play and that's a tough role in pointing out that the compromise of intellectual dynamism and moral vigour also brought in an eclipse of cultural glory and worse, the 'traditional value system'.

Here I came back to the importance of libraries in an intellectual build up of a society. I need to argue here forcefully that any kind of conflict resolutions cannot be attained without opening up the world mind-space. Libraries can play a crucial role if they are set up first and second made proper use of. The people of northeast India would gain access to windows opening into the world.

Why not we also resolve at this juncture that media organizations and other such bodies in the region can get together and try to set up a library at initial stage and then a study centre to harness effective people-to-people cooperation between the northeastern states and East Asian countries?

Otherwise, what is happening is that the 'rest of mainstream India' interposes itself between the northeast and the rest of the world. And because of bitterness towards the 'rest of India' obviously for all reasons – political to military interventions to counter insurgency – people develop a kind of hostility and suspicions towards all outsiders. Thus, first impression of Bangkok could be drug and something else and not the idyllic tourism. This is just to give an example.

On the other hand, people have grown vulnerable to western food courts like Pizza centres and different brands of burgers. So, we have a situation wherein natives in the region are getting only influenced by 'damaging ways' of western lifestyle. But who, other than media can take up the cudgel against such situations.

Media's role hereby increases manifold. A reporter should move out of his text-book definition of a 'fly on the wall' and get into the shoes of a social thinker. And, I need not tell you the incorrigible truth that: Thinkers in any society have to maintain the freedom of thinking!

To continue stressing on 'thinking' element in the media, there is perhaps also need to highlight total absence of a space to promote local literature in native dialects. I have tried to argue eloquently earlier that like any emerging societies, the North East has not able to reconcile divergent interest of communities, political aspirations and values. North East means different things to people of different ethnicities, tribes and social and economic classes. There is a room for extensive analyses of the political histories of different sets of people and their search for self-rule. Here I want to bring in literature more as an issue to ponder about.

It would not be out of place to refer here that Indian Urdu writers' initial response to India's partition was an outpouring of poems and fictions that were generally based on small-time characters or a writer's personal experience. But literature takes time to grow and that growth results in bringing in matured influence also on readers. Thus, my take is: the heart-wrenching pain of loss and displacement found space slowly. The media in north east needs to create such a space also that can anchor people's thinking and ideological values and at the same time keep the society rooted to its rich tradition.

In the ultimate, one must make a serious note that perhaps more than anything else this region does illustrate a peculiar combination of triumph and tragedy.

As I conclude, I do admit, north east India has made immense progress and so has the neighbouring countries with all limitations. Just like a protagonist of nationalism among Naga politicians, Hokishe Sema used to say: "staggeringly high achievements have been made, but staggering shortcomings too remain". This grey area is both the media's opportunity and hence also the responsibility.

In the end, I have tried to translate a few lines of a Hindi poem based on the teachings of Guru Nanak, which in English would read thus:

> 'Never exhibit only your sorrows,
>
> You need not test your luck too,
>
> What's yours will definitely be yours,
>
> You need not selfishly try to achieve that,
>
> This world is bound to change,
>
> It has always changed with those who dared to smile,
>
> My Friend, never try to look for an excuse to smile and
>
> Never Shirk your Job'.

Ends

Note:

This paper was presented by the author in a conference on *Media's Role in Facilitating Peace in Conflict Situation in Northeast India and Neighbouring Countries* organized by the Department of Mass Communication, Rajiv Gandhi University, Itanagar during 9-10 October 2014.

Advertising and Ethnicities: A Comparative Study of Sri Lanka and Northeast India

DARSHANA LIYANAGE

Ethnicity has become a key interest of advertisers in diverse societies. Contrary to the popular argument that ethnic identities are threatened by the intensified influence of media and consumer culture, they have become the core sites of representation and reproduction of ethnic identities. It is arguable that in today's (mass) mediated societies there are no ways of imagining ethnicities without the media's influence and impact on them. Advertising[1], no longer a mere commercial activity, is an important component of popular culture and hence plays a crucial part in the social and cultural life of our times. Sri Lanka[2] has long been a country of communal unrest, which culminated in a civil war. Northeast India is a region where a number of conflicting identities are in a constant battle of production and reproduction. The ways the ethnic identities are represented in advertisements in these two societies are worthy of studying in this context. When ad-makers segment a market for a particular brand, they mostly rely on ethnic identities. As a result, advertisements too become a site of reproduction of ethnic identities. This paper is intended to identify and analyze the ways of representations of ethnic identities in advertisements in Northeast India[3] and Sri Lanka by a comparative reading of a sample of print and electronic advertisements.

> On many occasions, clients have asked us to not take faces from northeast India stating that they do not represent the entire country and may end up confusing the viewers...Show me a regular ad film campaign where you have seen a north eastern face Ram Subramanian, founder and director Handloom Picture Company. (Tewari, 2014)

[F]or Sri Lankan advertising agencies, the issue is not balancing local ethnic types, but speaking to Sri Lankans by way of actors who are either Sri Lankan in a generic way or recognizably Sinhala. Steven Kemper (2001, p. 59)

Both in India and Sri Lanka advertising is probably the most visible multinational industry; in both countries, all most all the leading multinational advertising agencies are in operation. As such, no doubt, as an industry it plays a leading role in multinational capitalism. However, advertising is not only a business, industry, or a commercial activity but also a social, cultural, and political phenomenon as has been analyzed by many social and cultural theorists, ranging from Raymond Williams (2009) to Jean Baudrillard (2001). Despite being a multinational industry, advertising differs from country to country, region to region, allowing the construction of phrases like "European advertising", "US advertising", and "Indian advertising" etc. The country or regional specificities in advertising, is not a mere matter of country of origin but rather, deals with the different ways that the global is negotiated with the local in each country or region. Accordingly, advertising in any country, is about being global and local simultaneously. How advertising articulates ethnic ideologies in diverse societies is an important part of this local-global negotiation.

Sri Lanka has long been a country of communal unrest, which culminated in a civil war fought between the Liberation Tigers of Tamil Eelam (LTTE)[4] (which self-declared themselves the sole representatives of the Tamils[5] in Sri Lanka, after politically and militarily defeating the rival Tamil political/military groups), and the government forces. (For a detailed discussion on the ethnic crisis and civil war in Sri Lanka see: Tambiah, 1986; De Silva, 2012) DeVotta, 2004; Thiranagama, 2011.) The country now is facing the international community's demand for investigations on war crimes/human rights violations during the last phase of the war. Divided across the ethnic lines yet united by legislations and constitution, the country, after five years of the end of civil war, is still meandering without a proper vision and mechanism for post-war reconciliation. Moreover, the recent rise of ethno-religious fundamentalist groups and hate campaigns against the Muslim minority (for a detailed discussion see: Stein, 2014; Gugler, 2013; Senaratne, 2014) have casted a cloud over the peace and harmony in the country.

India also is a country of ethnic diversity and ethnic unrest. Especially, Northeast India is a land for different ethnic groups and "the Northeast", the "troubled periphery" (Bhaumik, 2009), "has been and continues to be a hotbed of ethnic, religious, linguistic and economic tension" (Barua, 2005, p. 231), now facing "insurgencies or separatist movements from over 50 groups...revolve around language and ethnicity, tribal rivalry, migration, control over local resources, access to water, and more significantly, a widespread feeling of exploitation and alienation from the Indian state" (Haokip, 2012, p. 222).

Given that both Sri Lanka and Northeast India are lands of contest of ethnic ideologies, senses and sentiments of self-respect and beyond that, right of separation and self-determination, the ideologies and violence of separatism versus national integration, make it interesting to study how advertising operates in these two lands. Also, how an industry of multinational capitalism links the global ways of consumption with the local ways of belongingness/alienation. As such, this paper intends to understand the ways in which ethnic ideologies are represented, negotiated, reconstructed, articulated, and contested in advertising in Sri Lanka and Northeast India. The focus of the paper is mainly on the most recent advertising campaigns, although it shuffle between historical examples and contemporary times for the betterment of the discussion. The secondary materials are used in contextualizing the socio-cultural relevance of advertising campaigns while a sample of advertisements is used as primary materials. In deciphering the meanings of selected advertisements a mixed method of textual reading, which includes the illuminations of semiotics, discourse analysis, hermeneutics and content analysis for the most part, is applied. As such, this is not a semiotic analysis or a discourse analysis of advertising per se. Rather, it emphasizes the importance of a mixed method textual reading, having freedom to go beyond the limit of a particular single method.

Advertising and Ethnicities

In a broader view, advertising, all over the world, shows two kinds of people: "people similar to us" and "people different from us". These two spans over all the models of representations like gender, class, ethnic, regional etc. Ethnic representation in advertising appears in three forms: the first, which targets the same ethnic group/s represented in, the second, which targets a different ethnic group/s than the represented, and the third, which targets to campaign across ethnicities. However, these three forms involve the subtle dichotomy of self/other, in which non-representation also becomes a way of representation. To segment a market on ethnic basis is "ethnic marketing/advertising" and to segment a market across the ethnic boundaries is "cross-cultural marketing/advertising". These two are the "targeted versus one voice" (Business and Finanace, 2011) that marketing/advertising practitioners debate on. Although this two models make sense as marketing/advertising strategies, it is not a simple matter of "targeted versus one" when it comes to the theme of representation.

Advertising that targets the same ethnic group/community that has been represented in the campaign is the most common type of ethnic representation in advertising. This involves with many forms such as featuring the people (including the celebrities) from a particular ethnic group, depicting culture specificities, lifestyles, etc. One common ethnic ad type is "copycat"[6] ads, which again can take many different forms. A radio jingle translated into a local language can reach a particular community not only passing the message but also giving the sense of being addressed by their own language. Print ads and television commercials (TVCs) that replace the originally used models with ethnic models are also types of copycat advertising.

Anthony J Cortse argues that the copycat advertising is ethnocentric as it "mistakenly assumes that African Americans and Latinos are simply dark-skinned white people" (2008, p. 96). This argument is sociologically valid as the "originals" always are the Whites (or the dominant groups/communities). However, as the question of representation does not involve only with the self (us) but also with the other (them), the copycat advertising brings an important dimension of ethnic representation. To put it simply, it may not be an apt response to the questions like "why them only?" and "why not us?" but, in case, to the question "why differently?" Although the issue of stereotyping is in the core of the academic discourse on representation, we should not ignore that the image of a community that it wants to see and show the other/s is always not "as it is", but rather "as it want to" or "according to its fantasy".

In fact, the copycat advertising is a primary model of ethnic advertising. The developed forms of ethnic advertising today engage with the ethnicity more complex and subtle ways. "Social reality" model as termed by Cortse (2008), attempts to bring a "true picture" of the ethnic group concerned, and beyond that links the feelings, attitudes, histories, of the community with brands. Here, ethnic advertising becomes more an active site of representation and reproduction of ethnic identities. Unlike in copycat advertising, this model is inseparable from market researches. As Roberta J. Astroff argues,

> "[T]exts" of market research can be analyzed and understood by analogy to ethnographies. They share the ethnographic text's nature as an "invention, not representation of cultures", and the result of a process of cultural production. Market researches produce a market by identifying, naming, and defining a culture as a market segment. (Astroff, 1994, p. 103)

Representation and reproduction have close ties; any attempt at representation is an attempt at reproduction. When an advertising campaign targets a particular ethnic group, representing them in the campaign and segments a market, it is, in fact, creating a market segment and reproducing ethnicity. In other words, both the market segment and the ethnicity are reproduced in the process of market segmenting for advertising. As a result, ethnic advertising that targets the same ethnic community represented/ reproduced in the campaign becomes not the outcome but the source of ethnic imagination. "If anthropology is understood as 'writing culture', what advertising 'writes' ends up producing culture" (Kemper, 2003, p. 52).

The second way in which advertising engages ethnicity is by depicting a particular ethnic group in a campaign, targeting a different ethnic group. This form is frequently criticized for stereotyping ethnic groups for the gaze and (sadistic, humiliating, sexist, etc.) pleasure of another (most of the time, the dominant) ethnic group. Nonetheless, the other side of the same coin, advertising that utilizes the supremacy (beauty/whiteness/ luxury) of a dominant ethnic group for the gaze and pleasure of another ethnic group, can also be taken as a sub category of this form. This is well observable in beauty and cosmetic, cigarettes and alcohol, automobile, and real estate and housing advertising in many countries.

The third form of ethnic advertising targets across ethnic boundaries while keeping ethnic representation as a matter of interest in the advertising campaign. Known as cross-cultural advertising, this category, perhaps, is getting more prominence in advertising in diverse societies. In a sense, it seems like using racial and ethnic prejudices for advertising is becoming old-fashioned while promoting ethnic harmony and respecting differences is becoming the new trend. Hence, it also seems like advertising has become the most prominent and practical site of multiculturalism with this form of multicultural advertising. Nevertheless, the criticism of multiculturalism gains much validity when it comes to this new trend of multicultural advertising. "By containing diversity in a common grid, multiculturalism preserves the ethnocentric paradigm of commodity relations that generate particularisms in the experience of life-worlds within transnational capitalism. Cultural difference sells" (San Juan, 2002, p. 347). As Slavoj Žižek argues, this is a postmodern or reflexive racism:

> Today's 'reflected' racism, however, is paradoxically able to articulate itself in terms of direct *respect* for the other's culture; was not the official argument for apartheid in the old South Africa that black culture should be preserved in its uniqueness , not dissipated in the Western melting-pot? Do not even today's European racists, like Le Pen, emphasizes how what they ask for is only the same right to cultural identity as Africans and others demand for themselves? (2000, p. 6)

As such, "the respect for differences" becomes disguised racism; "the fetishistic disavowal of cynicism: 'I know very well that all ethnic cultures are equal in value, yet, nevertheless, I will act as if mine is superior" (Myers, 2003). In his essay "Multiculturalism, Or, the Cultural Logic of Multinational Capitalism" Zizek declares:

> And, of course, the ideal form of ideology of this global capitalism is multiculturalism, the attitude which, from a kind of empty global position, treats each local culture the way the colonizer treats colonized people – as "natives" whose mores are to be carefully studied

and "respected."…In other words, multiculturalism is a disavowed, inverted, self-referential form of racism, a "racism with distance" – it respects the Other's identity, conceiving the Other as a self-enclosed, "authentic" community towards which he, the multiculturalist, maintains a distance rendered possible by privileged universal position…the multiculturalist respect for the Other's specificity is the very form of asserting one's own superiority. (Zizek, 1997, p. 44)

Unlike the earlier forms of "racist" advertising, the new form "respects the differences". This is best exemplified in advertising multinational fast food companies like McDonald and KFC. Nevertheless, the very process of these advertising campaigns transforms ethnicity to the "ethnic Thing", objectifying "the Other", reducing them to spectacles or objects. Again, what Zizek reminds us about multiculturalism well fits with this form of "multicultural advertising":

> The conflict about multiculturalism is already a conflict about *Leitkultur*[7]: it is not a conflict between cultures, but a conflict between different visions of how different cultures can and should coexist, about the rules and practices these cultures have to share if they are to coexist. (2012, p. 45)

Advertising and Ethnicity: Northeast India

Much has been written about "ethnicity in (the) Northeast India" (Agarawal, 1996; Hussain, 2004; Singh, 2008). Nonetheless, the problem lies in the core of the phrase making itself, which cannot be discussed within the limits of this paper. However, in short, "ethnicities" (despite of whether they fit into the academic definition of the concept or not) in the region as a multitude and "ethnicity" in the region as an entity, are to be problematized. Do the two women hockey players in *Chak de! India* (2007) represent an ethnic identity (of the Northeast) or a regional identity? Or, as in the most recent case of Mary Kom, does she represent an ethnic identity (of the Northeast) or a regional identity? Where does the line between ethnicity and regionality in the Northeast lay; first, for the people in the region, and second, for the people outside the region?

Perhaps, cement advertising in the region is the prime site of ethnic representation that targets the ethnic groups in the region itself. The reason behind this can be that cement being a regional product often targets a local market. Nonetheless, given the multiplicity of the ethnic identities of the region, it is a difficult task for marketers/ advertisers to segment the markets along the ethnic lines. The only exception is outdoor advertising (and to some extends print advertising too, given that the local language newspapers have a considerable readership), which is cheaper in comparison to the print and electronic advertising. (The most noted case here is the Surya cement's "Build fresh and Strong Assam" campaign, which targeted a single state and arguably, a single "ethnic" group too.) That is the reason behind local advertising agencies mostly depend on outdoor advertising while print and electronic advertising in the region are mostly designed by the major advertising agencies outside the region (defiantly, in the metropolises).

Mostly electronic advertisements that appear in local languages are dubbed in local languages (that too by non-local people) and regionally distributed. Although one can argue whether it comes under the advertising proper or not, the music video produced for Star cement (Srinivasan, 2010) is a pioneer work in this regional segmenting and regional representation targeted the region itself. The music video brought together four celebrities from four states of the region (along with one from the mainstream) to sing a multilingual song with the theme "our Northeast our Star". Its appeal is to the development sentiments; portraying a positive picture of building Northeast (with cement). The music video is a collage of northeast's ethnicities and cultures (although not each and every). Interestingly, the metaphor of collage is more suitable as it at the same time a whole as Northeast but clearly depicts differences too; differences are alive within the whole. This is very evident in the way those celebrities were separately used as a part of the campaign, especially in print media. For example, continued use of the cultural icon Bupen Hazarika (even after his death) in advertising Star cement, addresses different people and different sentiments at different levels.

An advanced step of ethno-regional segmenting is well exemplified in the Dalmia cement advertising campaign for its Northeast launch in 2013. If Star cement used four figures to represent the ethnic identities of the region, Dalmia focused on a single figure, Mary Kom, to represent the region and the people of the region and hence to segment the Northeast cement market. (For a detailed discussion on Dalmia cement campaign see: Esse & Liyanage, 2014).

The incredible India advertising campaign's depiction of the Northeast India (Nair, 2014) is one of the best examples of bringing ethnicity to the field of advertising, by the other and for the other (the campaign targeted both the international and domestic tourist markets). There is a politics of phrase making, as it is a way and act of naming, projecting, manipulating, and even dominating. "Paradise unexplored" was the tagline that appeared in the advertisements. The question is, what really is unexplored in this "paradise"? As the visuals in the advertisements prove it is not only the land and the nature but the people and cultures too. Underlying this "unexplored" is the idea of "underdeveloped' or less civilized as Duncan McDui-Ra argues:

> Images of tribal and other ethnic groups in tourism campaigns both construct and reflect dominant ways of seeing Northeast people. The portrayal of the Northeast for the tourism market reflects the three 'un' myths discussed by Echtner and Prasad (2003) in their analysis of the ways Third World destinations are represented to foreigners: 'unchanged', 'unrestrained', and 'uncivilized'. Interestingly, in the case of the Northeast, these 'un' myths not only cater for foreign tourists but to the enormous domestic tourism market. (McDuie-Ra, 2012, p. 92)

If one reads the texts of the incredible India advertising campaign for the Northeast in comparison to the texts of the campaign for metropolis in the "incredible India" full campaign, this is very evident. As such, this branding of the Northeast as the "paradise unexplored", not only brings the old wine in new bottles, but at the same time, beyond that, exemplifies how multiculturalism operates as a postmodern racism, asserting that "you are different. I respect your difference (but you are unexplored)". The cynicism at its highest comes out; "the unexplored" is to be "explored" by (an outside) "explorer"! Here we witness, what Zizek (1997) terms as the "ethnic Thing...objectification of the Other". This objectification is not the old racist objectification but a multicultural objectification:

Multiculturalism is a racism which empties its own position of all positive content (the multiculturalist is not a direct racist, he doesn't oppose to the Other the particular values of his own culture), but nonetheless retains this position as the privileged empty point of universality from which one is able to appreciate (and depreciate) properly other particular cultures[.] (1997, p. 45)

A recent television commercial (TVC) for Nestle (Nirvana Films, 2014) with the tagline "when goodness is shared over food life smiles", is another good example of multicultural advertising, and hence objectification of the Northeast ethnicity. "We went with a girl from the Northeast, an area we usually don't cast from, for I think we should break stereotypes" (Bareu, 2014) the South Asia president of the advertising agency who created the commercial said to the media. The advertisement shows how the hostile attitude of a little boy towards his adopted sister changes as they start sharing food. As shown in the commercial, the family is urban middle class and Hindi speaking and the adopted girl child is from the Northeast. The advertisement, on one level, is an attempt to exploit the anti-discrimination discourse and activism, and on another, brings the notion of "sharing" as a way of changing attitudes and relations. However, a deeper reading of the advertisement generates multitude meanings. The adopted child, being a girl, inter-texts the commercial with the social and media discourse of human trafficking, the idea that the Northeast is one of the regions infamous for human trafficking, and then, necessarily with the ideas of poverty and underdevelopment, which goes well with the theme of "sharing food".

Metaphorically, the ad is depicting the Northeast as the adopted child of "mainland family", as the girl is adopted to the urban middle class Hindi speaking family, so the Northeast to the mainland. As such, the ad places itself in the dominant discourse of national integration and its way of articulating the minorities or the marginalized communities, be it the "good" "patriotic" Muslim, or the "adopted child", or any other "someone". The integration does not mean different communities getting together to make one entity, but, rather, the way others place in the mainstream. The adopted girl child climbs trees, collects earthworms into bottle, steals food, and hence gains the curios interest of her brother. As it appeared in the media, "the client particularly wanted an oriental-looking child" (Tewari, 2014). One interesting aspect here is that in the popular "the Northeast" discourses there is a regional/ethnic resemblance. To represent the northeast is not just to represent a region but an ethnicity. In popular discourse, for the mainland, the Northeast is homogeneity, which can be trimmed down to one single ethnicity. This misconception highly depends on the physical features rather than cultural differences, and hence closer to race than ethnicity.

The TVC for the KBC 2014 launch (SET India, 2014) which is a brilliant example of advertising that simultaneously targets both the represented and other. The advertisement shows a young girl from the Northeast contesting in the popular television game show, been asked to name the country where Kohima is situated. She is given four options; China, Nepal, India, and Bhutan. The girl opts for an audience poll. The scene in the studio is parallel cuts to different audiences watching the show on the television; a family (most probably the family of the contestant), three waiters (among them one a Northeast Indian), two security guards (one a Northeast Indian), and two chefs (one a Northeast Indian). When she opts for an audience poll the viewers, who represent the "mainland" laughs at her as if she is ignorant of such a simple fact, while the viewers, who represent the Northeast, seem embarrassed about not only her ignorance but people's ignorance of the region. When the quizzer, Bollywood superstar Amitabh Bachchan[8], announces the results of the audience poll that 100 per cent has the answer India and everyone knows it, the contestant replies, "yes everyone knows that but how many acknowledge it", sending a shocking message to the audience. Moreover, her response makes the embarrassed party relieved and the humiliating party embarrassed and hence their position and roles are reversed, which can broadly be read as a role change of "mainlanders" and "Northeasterners". The commercial plays a hide-and-seek game over truths and lies, knowns and unknowns. In fact, the commercial is reflexive as the question itself is against the 100 per cent audience poll's result that Kohima is in India. In the commercial, the contestant, Kohima, and Northeasterners watching the show on TV, are on one side, while the quizzer and rest are on the other side, polarized though the line of being or non-being in India. It is interesting as shown in the advertisement the "mainlanders" accept it as a matter of fact when the girl counter questions, "How many acknowledge it?"

The campaign for vim bar featuring the "world's largest family" from Mizoram (VimIndia, Sabse Badi Family, Sabse Tez Vim, 2014; VimIndia, Breakfast with World's Largest Family, 2014; VimIndia, Football with the Family, 2014; VimIndia, 160 Birthdays, 1 Family: Sabse Tez Vim, 2014; VimIndia, Lunch with the World's Largest Family!, 2014) is, again, about the Northeasterner, "the stranger". A Bollywood celebrity visits the largest family to introduce the particular brand to them. The campaign shows something "strange" from the Northeast to the mainland.

The Tata Salt advertising campaign featuring Mary Kom has applied a new technique of ethnic representation. On one level, as done in Dalmia, cement campaign, tries to depict Mary Kom as a single figure that can represent an ethnic entity. However, beyond that, on the other level, it tries to negotiate this particular "ethnic figure" with the "generic Indian figure", which makes the whole campaign double positioned both in the nationality discourse and in the Northeast discourse simultaneously. The TVCs in the campaign mixes up scenes from movie and hence takes the advantage of the filmic transformation of Mary Kom to Priyanka Chopra.

For a long, the Northeast remained untouched by the advertising industry and was considered unsuitable for the "generic Indian" model of advertising. However, the recent interest of the industry in the region has made a new way of negotiation and contest of ethnic identities in the region. The Northeast was made a "frontier" by the British, then a "political and administrative entity" by the Indian State, then "an object of study" by the academic and media discourse, and now it is the time it is being made "a brand" by the advertising industry.

Advertising and Ethnicity: Sri Lanka

In Sri Lanka, all the leading advertising agencies are in Colombo capital, which stands for the political and ideological power of the Sinhala majority. (To put the civil war in a metaphor, it was a south (Colombo) versus north (Jaffna) war, as such.) Accordingly, "Colombo products" are predominantly Sinhala products. As Steven Kemper rightly argues,

[T]he striking character of Sri Lankan life is the near invisibility of Tamils in Sri Lankan public culture. The occasional advertisement aims at a Tamil audience, but the general assumption that Sri Lankan culture is Sinhala culture is replicated in Sri Lankan advertising practice. (2001, p. 59)

The representation of the "generic Sri Lankan" in advertising in Sri Lanka is a matter of appearing as Sinhala than really being Sinhala. In fact, as Kemper reveals, the majority of the models used in advertising in 1990s were Burghers and Tamil male models overrepresented the industry. Moreover, not only Muslims and Bohras (a Shi'a Muslim community from Bombay, famous for their business success) appeared in Sri Lankan advertisements, in some cases, advertisements were produced in India using Indian models. The ethnic identity of the model was not a problem as far as he or she fits with figure of the "generic Sri Lankan". "To cap off the irony, when Sri Lankan consumers look at newsprint and television, they see these models – whether they are Muslim, Tamil, Burgher, or Sinhala- as, 'sophisticated Sinhala'" (2001, p. 67). Although, now the ethnic composition in advertising industry has changed, still this remains a reality.

Nevertheless, advertising is not a mere matter of faces and figures that appear in, rather, the ideologies it negotiates, articulates, and reconstructs through those faces and figures. While the faces and figures used in advertising themselves are ideologically embedded, advertising in Sri Lanka, during the war period, and especially, celebrating the victory over LTTE, as all other sites of dominant cultural production, was a part and parcel of, both as an agent of and respondent to, dominant ethnic ideologies and war-mentality[9]. One good example is the increased usage of "lion" symbol in advertising. The lion is the symbol that represents the Sinhala people. Although it symbolizes the nation too, appearing in the national flag, in popular discourse lions are Sinhala people. In fact, in another metaphor, the war was between "lions" and "tigers". It is ambiguously used both for the nationality and for Sinhala people; for example, Sri Lankan cricket team is often referred as *"sinha patawu"* (lion cubs) regardless of the fact that players belong to different ethnic communities. Interestingly, one advertising campaign for recruiting the soldiers to Sri Lankan army, which is predominantly a Sinhala force with four regiments named after Sinhala royalty, came with the tagline *"sinha patawunge paradisya"* (Lion cubs' paradise) (De Mel, 2007, p. 72). The recurrence of lion symbol in advertising campaigns in Sri Lanka hence is highly ethno-ideological. Other than the lion symbol, there are a number of ethno-religious symbols that recur in advertisements in Sri Lanka, which include ancient cities, paddy fields, ancient reservoirs etc.

During the war, some advertising campaigns explicitly supported war and dominant ethnic ideologies;

> [I]n a full-page advertisement taken out by MAS Holdings, a leading business group in the transnational apparel industry based in Colombo. On 7 June 2000, which was declared War Hero's Day by the Peoples' Alliance government, it took out a full-page advertisement depicting an idle sword leaning on a jakfruit with the question/slogan 'Is the sword that is not for war, for chopping jakfruit?' A verse in the advertisement warned the public that the time for idleness was over and that duty demanded all acts of terror be punished. In its singular address to the Sinhala public (it appeared in Sinhala even when published in the English language *Daily News*) and the referents of farmer, poet, monk and mother (icons of a circulating popular Sinhala culture), all of whom nurture the war hero, the Tamil and Muslim ethnic other remained a structuring absence. (De Mel, 2007, p. 84)

As De Mel cites, following the February 2002 Memorandum of Understanding signed by the then government of Sri Lanka and LTTE, and the ceasefire, some corporate advertisements appeared with the taglines such as "As peace enter Jaffna so we do!", "Mother, now you're not alone in Jaffna", and "Now Jaffna is in our net" (2007, p. 85). These advertisements reflect the view that Jaffna as a territory regained. She further argues that the advertising industry celebrated the (temporary) peace in highly charged militaristic language. Some of the taglines as she cites are; "In times of war the only weapon you need is talent", "Warning explosive ideas inside", "Graveyard for bombed ideas", and "Back with bang!" (2007, p. 85). Further, she argues;

War, as instrumentally used in these advertisements, was merely a witty punchline, its condition brought to us devoid of its substance. But the political economy of the sign of war, kept alive by the advertisements seemingly harmlessly in this way, had a use and exchange value that made war an available option during difficult peace negotiations if necessary, and a series of advertisements by the mobile phone operator Dialog GSM kept to this circulating economy/ narrative of the *preparedness* for war. As chief sponsor of the Sri Lankan army's rugby squad, one of Dialogue GSM's advertisements depicted pictures from a rugby match and locker room as precise military-like manoeuvres on and off the field.54Another in the series portrayed a memo with details of the squad's game plan ratified with a seal stating in bold letters, 'Attack approved.' In this quotidianness of battle even during the ceasefire, the corporate sector played a key role in mediating war and peace as a militaristic continuum: the seduction of this trajectory precisely in its masking of the alliance between national security and global capital. (2007, p. 85)

Some advertising campaigns launched during the high time of war and celebrating the victory over the LTTE clearly depicts how the dominant ethnic ideologies and global capital converge. Depicting the military as "the saviors of the nation" and "*rana wiruwo*" (war heroes), was a common theme that brought into advertising campaigns (Heensare, 2009; 24frameslk, 2009). One among many programmes launched to hero-warship the military, "*ranawiru* real star", a reality TV show, was sponsored by corporate advertising (DialogAxista, 2010).

Advertising in Sri Lanka, thus, has been and is continuing to be reflection of mono-ethnic national identity. Although there are rare examples of minorities represented in advertising, they too have subtexts of mono-ethnic nationality.

Conclusions

Advertising in Sri Lanka and Northeast India exemplify two distinct ways of negotiating ethnic ideologies. In Sri Lanka, advertising is more direct in its mono-ethnic model and in Northeast India, the new trend is multicultural advertising as evident by the recent interest in the region shown by ad-makers. However, both the forms are in line with the logic of global capitalism; in one context cultural dominancy sells while in the other cultural differences sell. In both cases, despite of the matter of visibility or non-visibility in advertising, the Other is an "ethnic Thing". If the former is direct racism, the latter is "racism with a distance". In the former context, the Other is the enemy, and in the latter the Other is the "folkloric spectacle" (Žižek, 1997, p. 44). In both cases, advertising is a site of ethnic ideologies too.

Notes

1   Although, "advertising" is a vaguely used word to refer to a number of activities and stuffs, my focus here is only on the corporate display advertising/ advertisements.

2   This refers to the nation island of 65610 km2 with a population of 20.23 MM and situated in the Indian Ocean, below the southern tip of India. However, note that my use of the term does not mean a social or cultural homogeneity, as my focus will mostly be on the Sinhala dominated areas of the country.

3   I will be using two terms in this paper; "Northeast" and "the Northeast". By the first I refer to the "geographical area" (which is legitimized by"[t]he political process and 'administrative convenience' " (Shimray, 2004) that covers the eight states; Arunachal Pradesh, Assam, Manipur, Meghalaya, Mizoram, Nagaland, Sikkim, and Tripura. By the second, I refer to the discursive construct of "the Northeast" as a socio-economic and cultural entity.

4   The demand of Tamils for political power appeared in different forms in post-colonial Sri Lanka. However, the shift from demand for a federal state to demand for separate state was the crucial turning point. LTTE was the strongest militant group, which fought for the cause of a separate state in Tamil Eelam (the areas that covers northern and eastern parts of Sri Lanka) with a huge military and militant power that included suicide bombers.

5   The ethnic composition of population in Sri Lanka is as follows: Sinhalese 74.88%, Sri Lankan Tamils 11.21%, Sri Lankan Moors 9.23%, Indian Tamils 5.16, Malay 0.20, Burghers 0.18, others 0.14 (source: (Census of Population

and Housing - 2012, 2012). The Indian Tamils, who are the descendants South Indian labourers brought by the British to work on the coffee and later on the tea plantations and live in the central highlands of the country, did not directly engaged in militant activities (Bass, 2013). They depend on trade union derived political parties for bargaining their demands.

6   Anthony J. Cortse uses the term for "an ad using a white model is duplicated with a black or Latino model" (2008, p. 95).

7   The dominant culture.

8   Ironically this is the same superstar who made a mistake tweeting "Mary Kom!! wins boxing bout, insured (sic) a Bronze! What a story! A Mother of two from Assam, creates moment of pride for India!!", for which he apologized later (Karmakar, 2012).

9   "Mindset" is a buzzword used in advertising and marketing, which refers to a particular ways of thinking of a community.

References

24frameslk. (2009, May 7). *YouTube*. Retrieved September 6, 2014, from Mobitel SIM Registration Advertisement: http://www.youtube.com/watch?v=xSxbWbAAE-A

Agarawal, M. (Ed.). (1996). *Ethnicity, Nationalism, and Culture in North-East India*. New Delhi: Indus Publishing Company.

Astroff, R. J. (1994). Advertising, Anthropology, and Cultural Brokers: A Research Report. In B. G. Englis (Ed.), *Global and Multinational Advertisng* (pp. 103-113). New Jersey: Lawrence Eralbaum Associates.

Bareu, E. (2014, September 10). *Coca-Cola & Dabbawala campaigns among McCann's best works*. Retrieved September 10, 2014, from The Economic Times: http://economictimes.indiatimes.com/magazines/brand-equity/coca-cola-dabbawala-campaigns-among-mccanns-best-works/articleshow/42107692.cms?prtpage=1

Barua, P. P. (2005). *The State at War in South Asia.* Lincoln: University of Nebraska Press.

Baruah, S. (2003). Citizens and Denizens: Ethnicity, Homeland, and the Crisis of Displacement in Northeast India. *Journal of Refugee Studies, 16*(1), 44-66.

Bass, D. (2013). *Everyday Ethnicity in Sri Lanka: Up-Country Tamils Identity Politics.* London and New York: Routledge.

Baudrillard, J. (2001). *Jean Baudrillard: Selected Writings.* (M. Poster, Ed.) California: Stanford University Press.

Bhaumik, S. (2009). *Troubled Periphery: Crisis of India's North East.* New Delhi: Sage Publications.

Business and Finanace. (2011, December 31). Retrieved September 1, 2014, from The Economist: http://www.economist.com/node/21542203

Census of Population and Housing - 2012. (2012). Retrieved September 1, 2014, from Department of Census and Statistics - Sri Lanka: http://www.statistics.gov.lk/PopHouSat/CPH2012Visualization/htdocs/index.php?usecase=indicator&action=Data&indId=11

Chopra, A. (Producer), Sahni, J. (Writer), & Amin, S. (Director). (2007). *Chak de! India* [Motion Picture]. India: Yash Raj Films.

Cortse, A. J. (2008). *Provocateur: Images of Women and Minorities in Advertisng* (3rd ed.). Lanham: Rowman and Littlefield Publishers Inc.

De Mel, N. (2007). *Militarizing Sri Lanka: Popular Culture, Memory and Narrative in the Armed Conflict.* New Delhi: Sage Publications.

De Silva, K. M. (2012). *Sri Lanka and the Defeat of the LTTE .* New Delhi: Penguin Books India.

DeVotta, N. (2004). *Blowback: Linguistic Nationalism, Institutional Decay, and Ethnic Conflict in Sri Lanka.* Stanford: Stanford University Press.

DialogAxista. (2010, November 14). *YouTube.* Retrieved September 5, 2014, from Ranaviru Real Star [TVC]: http://www.youtube.com/

watch?v=U4oh8GfrJmI

Echtner, C., & Prasad, P. (2003). The Concept of Third World Tourism Marketing. *Annals of Tourism Research, 30*(3), 660-682.

Esse, D., & Liyanage, D. (2014, May). "Our Kommitment to the Nation": Where Mary Kom (Identity) Meets Dalmia Cement (Development/ Market). *Asian Journal of Research in Social Sciences and Humanities, 4*(5), 663-672.

Gugler, T. K. (2013). *Südasien-Chronik/South Asia Chronicle.* Retrieved September 1, 2014, from Buddhist Zion: Sri Lanka's Sinhalisation Politics toward its Muslim Minority: http://edoc.hu-berlin.de/suedasien/band-3/161/PDF/161.pdf

Haokip, G. T. (2012). On Ethnicity and Development Imperative: A Case Study of North-East India. *Asian Ethnicity, 13*(3), 217-228.

Heensare. (2009, August 21). *Dialog GSM - Uththamachara.* Retrieved September 6, 2014, from YouTube: http://www.youtube.com/ watch?v=wjI1Bb49PO8

Hussain, M. (2004). Nationalities, Ethnic Process, and Violence in India's Northeast. In R. Samaddar (Ed.), *Peace Studies: An Introduction to the Concept, Scope, and Themes* (pp. 292-318). New Delhi: Sage Publications India Ltd.

Johari, A. (2014, June 18). *Ad Trend.* Retrieved September 4, 2014, from Scroll.in: http://scroll.in/article/667254/Indian-advertisements-slowly-begin-to-include-people-from-the-North-East

Karmakar, R. (2012, August 8). *Amitabh Bachchan's tweet on Mary Kom angers northeast.* Retrieved September 6, 2014, from Hindustantimes: http://www.hindustantimes.com/Specials/Sports/Olympics2012/ Chunk-HT-UI-Olympics-OtherStories/Amitabh-Bachchan-s-tweet-on-Mary-Kom-angers-northeast/SP-Article10-910156.aspx

Kemper, S. (2001). *Buying and Believing: Sri Lankan Advertisnig and Consumers in a Transnational World.* Chicago: The University of Chicago Press.

Darshana Liyanage

Kemper, S. (2003). How Advertisng Makes its Object. In T. d. Malefyte, & B. Moeran (Eds.), *Advertising Cultures* (pp. 35-54). Oxford and New York: Berg.

McDuie-Ra, D. (2012). *Northeast Migrants in Delhi: Race, Refuge, and Retail.* Amsterdam: Amsterdam University Press.

Myers, T. (2003). *Slavoj Žižek - Key Ideas.* Retrieved September 2, 2014, from lacan.com: http://www.lacan.com/zizekchro1.htm

Nair, R. (2014, February 14). *Incredible India North East 90 sec.* Retrieved September 6, 2014, from YouTube: https://www.youtube.com/watch?v=QXCmCY1rid8

NirvanaFilms. (2014, March 7). *Nestlé.* Retrieved September 7, 2014, from YouTube: http://www.youtube.com/watch?v=e8-pSGN1_ec

San Juan, E. J. (2002). *Racism and Cultural Studies: Critique of Multiculturalist Ideology and and the Politics of Difference.* Durham: Duke University Press.

Senaratne, K. (2014, April 15). *The 'Mad Monk' Phenomenon: BBS as the underside of Sinhala-Buddhism.* Retrieved September 1, 2014, from GroundViews: http://groundviews.org/2014/04/15/the-mad-monk-phenomenon-bbs-as-the-underside-of-sinhala-buddhism/

SETIndia. (2014, July 8). *KBC 2014 launch film - Kohima.* Retrieved September 7, 2014, from YouTube: http://www.youtube.com/watch?v=QVLyDOW2jC8

Shimray, U. (2004). Socio-Political Unrest in the Region Called North-East India. *Economic and Political Weekly, 39*(42), 4637-4643.

Singh, A. (2008). Ethnic Diversity, Autonomy, and Territoriality in Northeast India: A Case of Tribal Autonomy in Assam. *Strategic Analysis, 32*(26), 1101-1114.

Srinivasan, R. (2010, December 25). *Star North-East.mp4.* Retrieved September 7, 2014, from YouTube: http://www.youtube.com/watch?v=t__tSesem78

Stein, S. (2014, February 14). *Interreligious Tension in South and Southeast Asia*. Retrieved September 1, 2014, from CSS: http://www.css.ethz.ch/publications/pdfs/CSSAnalyses148-EN.pdf

Tambiah, S. J. (1986). *Sri Lanka: Ethnic Fratricide and Dismatling of Dimocracy*. London: I.B Tauris & Co Ltd.

Tewari, S. (2014, July 15). *KBC Kohima: Winning hearts*. Retrieved September 3, 2014, from Afaqs!: http://www.afaqs.com/news/story/41368_KBC-Kohima:-Winning-Hearts

Thiranagama, S. (2011). *In My Mother's House: Civil War in Sri Lanka*. Philadelphia: University of Pennsylvania Press.

VimIndia. (2014, February 15). *160 Birthdays, 1 Family: Sabse Tez Vim*. Retrieved September 6, 2014, from YouTube: http://www.youtube.com/watch?v=qo_emCnZTBE&index=3&list=UUKN6LUsHc9YjUvK0TcaubHA

VimIndia. (2014, February 15). *Breakfast for 160 Members*. Retrieved September 6, 2014, from YouTube: http://www.youtube.com/watch?v=RJkkOZhkUbU&index=4&list=UUKN6LUsHc9YjUvK0TcaubHA

VimIndia. (2014, February !7). *Breakfast with World's Largest Family*. Retrieved September 5, 2014, from YouTube: http://www.youtube.com/watch?v=O7kSfQ0XOPw&index=1&list=UUKN6LUsHc9YjUvK0TcaubHA

VimIndia. (2014, February 15). *Football with the Family*. Retrieved September 6, 2014, from YouTube: http://www.youtube.com/watch?v=9S_nvnRMqys&list=UUKN6LUsHc9YjUvK0TcaubHA&index=2

VimIndia. (2014, February 15). *Lunch with the World's Largest Family!* Retrieved September 6, 2014, from YouTube: http://www.youtube.com/watch?v=sDqCFNs7bV0&index=6&list=UUKN6LUsHc9YjUvK0TcaubHA

VimIndia. (2014, February 11). *Sabse Badi Family, Sabse Tez Vim*. Retrieved September 6, 2014, from YouTube: http://www.youtube.com/

watch?v=9DvwUB6KT0s

Williams, R. (2009). Advertising: The Magic System. In J. Turow, & M. P. McAllister, *The Advertising and Consumer Culture Reader* (pp. 13 – 24). New York and London: Routledge.

Žižek, S. (1997, September-October). Multiculturalism, Or. the Cultural Logic of Multinational Capitalism. *New Left Review, I*(225), 28-51.

Žižek, S. (2000). *The Fragile Absolute: Or, Why is the Christian Legacy Worth Fighting for.* London and New York: Verso.

Žižek, S. (2012). *The Year of Dreaming Dangerously.* London and Brooklyn: Verso.

www.ingramcontent.com/pod-product-compliance
Lightning Source LLC
Chambersburg PA
CBHW060836100426

42814CB00016B/403/J